As a Man Thinketh, Volume 2

AS A MAN THINKETH, VOLUME 2

JAMES ALLEN

Selected and Edited by James H. Fedor,

MindArt
Bountiful, Utah

MindArt Publishing
P.O. Box 641
Bountiful, Utah 84010

Library of Congress Catalog Card Number
88-62350

ISBN 0-929896-00-9

MindArt books are available at special discounts for bulk purchases for sales promotions, premiums, fund-raising, or educational use.
For details, contact:

Special Sales Director
MindArt Publishing
P.O. Box 641
Bountiful, Utah 84010

10 9 8 7 6 5 4 3 2 1

Printed in the United States of America

Cover design by James H. Fedor

Dedication

The compiler dedicates this volume to his parents, Joseph and Joan, who taught him the principles in this book by practical example; to Wayne Wride who first introduced him to James Allen's original *As a Man Thinketh*; and finally to James Allen himself who, although removed from the compiler by almost a century and the worlds that may lay between them, has nonetheless guided and shaped the compiler's life.

Introduction

James Allen was born in 1864 in Leicester County in Central England near Birmingham. He worked most of his adult life as an administration assistant to several British manufacturers. In 1902, just over 9 years before his death in early 1912, he decided to retire from the hustle and bustle of industrial life and devote himself to writing and finding the principles by which all men could find inner peace and happiness. In the brief last years of his life, James Allen produced nineteen books which would guide later generations in numerous nations with a rich outpouring of inspiration.

After publishing his first book, *From Poverty to Power*, in 1907, Allen and his wife Lily moved to Ilfracombe on England's southwest coast. There he led a quiet but productive life of meditation and reflection. Allen drank deeply from the wisdom found in the Bible but also gained much enlightenment from the holy books of the Far East. From his hours of study, personal meditation at the seaside, and his favorite pastime, gardening, Allen's mind was fertile ground for a life of the spirit. He wrote, "A noble and Godlike character is not a thing of favor or chance, but is the direct result of continued effort in right-thinking, the effect of long-cherished associations with Godlike thoughts." Allen had discovered for himself the principle that, "A man cannot be separated from his mind. His life cannot be separated from his thoughts. Mind, thought, and life are as inseparable as light, radiance, and color....It follows that deliberately to change the thoughts is to change the man."

It was deep, poignant thoughts such as these that made one of his books so enduring—*As Man Thinketh* has been considered by many to be the "grandaddy" of modern inspirational literature. It would be difficult, if not impossible, to determine just how many people have been touched by this one book, *As a Man Thinketh.* It is now being printed by dozens of publishing companies in English-speaking countries and has been translated into many foreign languages as well. It has been printed in hardback, softback, small pocket-sized editions, included in combination with other inspirational works and has also been recorded on audiocassette. Being so widely published, conservative attempts to determine how many volumes have been sold number into the millions.

Although millions of readers may be acquainted with James Allen's *As a Man Thinketh*, few are aware of his 18 other books which mostly deal with the same subject of enriching the inner mental environment and which are every bit as inspiring. The book that you now hold in your hands, *As a Man Thinketh, Volume 2,* is a compilation of choice selections from James Allen's other books. This volume is an entirely new book and duplicates nothing from the original *As a Man Thinketh* and yet comes from the same inspired teacher, James Allen, and amplifies further on Allen's original theme that we are what we think. Only minor editing has been done to Americanize the spelling with a few word changes for the modern reader's benefit thus preserving as much as possible the original spirit of Allen's writing.

Table of Contents

CHAPTER 1

Thought and Action

*Guard well your thoughts, reader, for what
you really are in your secret thoughts today,
be it good or evil, you will, sooner or later,
become in actual deed.*

As the fruit to the tree and the water to the spring, so is action to thought. It does not come into manifestation suddenly and without a cause. It is the result of a long and silent growth, the end of a hidden process which has long been gathering force. The fruit of the tree and the water gushing from the rock are both the effect of a combination of natural processes in air and earth which have long worked together in secret to produce the phenomenon; and the beautiful acts of enlightenment and the dark deeds of sin are both the ripened effects of trains of thought which have long been harbored in the mind.

The sudden falling, when greatly tempted, into some grievous sin by one who was believed, and who probably believed himself, to stand firm is seen neither to be a *sudden* nor a causeless thing when the hidden processes of thought which led up to it are revealed. The *falling* was merely the end, the outworking, the finished result of what commenced in the mind probably years before. The man had allowed a wrong thought to enter his mind, and a second and a third time he had welcomed it and allowed it to nestle in his heart. Gradually he became accustomed to it, and cherished, and fondled, and tended it; and so it grew, until at last it attained such strength and force that it attracted to itself the opportunity which enabled it to burst forth and ripen into act. As falls the stately building whose foundations have been gradually undermined by the action of water, so at last falls the strong man who allows corrupt thoughts to creep into his mind and secretly undermine his character.

When it is seen that all sin and temptation are the natural outcome of the thoughts of the individual, the way to overcome sin and temptation becomes plain, and its achievement a near possibility, and, sooner or later, a certain reality; for if a man will admit, cherish, and brood upon thoughts that are pure and good, those thoughts, just as surely as the impure, will grow and gather force and will at last attract to themselves the opportunities which will enable them to ripen into act.

"There is nothing hidden that shall not be revealed," and every thought that is harbored in the mind must, by virtue of the impelling force which is inherent in the universe, at last blossom into acts good or bad according to its nature. The divine Teacher and the sensualist are both the product of their own thoughts and have become what they are as the result of the seeds of thought which they have implanted, or allowed to fall, into the garden of the heart and have afterwards watered, tended, and cultivated.

Let no man think he can overcome sin and temptation by wrestling with opportunity; he can only overcome them by purifying his thoughts; and if he will, day by day, in the silence of his soul, and in the performance of his duties, strenuously overcome all erroneous inclination, and put in its place thoughts that are true and that will endure the light, opportunity to do evil will give place to opportunity for accomplishing good; for a man can only attract that to him which is in harmony with his nature, and no temptation can gravitate to a man unless there is that in his heart which is capable of responding to it.

Guard well your thoughts, reader, for what you really *are* in your secret thoughts today, be it good or evil, you will, sooner or later, *become* in actual deed. He who unwearyingly guards the portals of his mind against the intrusion of sinful thoughts, and occupies himself with loving thoughts, with pure, strong, and beautiful thoughts, will when the season of their ripening comes, bring forth the fruits of gentle and holy deeds, and no temptation that can come against him shall find him unarmed or unprepared.

Note: This chapter originally printed as Chapter 9 in <u>Above Life's Turmoil</u>.

CHAPTER 2

Your Dominant Mental Attitude

Every impure and selfish thought that you send out comes back to you in your circumstances in some form of suffering; every pure and unselfish thought returns to you in some form of blessedness. Your circumstances are effects of which the cause is inward and invisible.

As a being of thought, your dominant mental attitude will determine your condition in life. It will also be the gauge of your knowledge and the measure of your attainment. The so-called limitations of your nature are the boundary lines of your thoughts; they are self-erected fences and can be drawn to a narrower circle, extended to a wider, or be allowed to remain.

You are the thinker of your thoughts, and as such you are the maker of yourself and condition. Thought is causal and creative, and appears in your character and life in the form of *results*. There are no accidents in your life. Both its harmonies and antagonisms are the responsive echoes of your thoughts. A man thinks, and his life appears.

If your dominant mental attitude is peaceable and lovable, bliss and blessedness will follow you; if it be resistant and hateful, trouble and distress will cloud your pathway. Out of ill-will will come grief and disaster; out of goodwill, healing and reparation.

You imagine your circumstances as being separate from yourself, but they are intimately related to your thought world. Nothing appears without an adequate cause. Everything that happens is just. Nothing is fated, everything is formed.

As you think, you travel; as you love, you attract. You are today where your thoughts have brought you; you will be tomorrow where your thoughts take you. You cannot escape the result of your thoughts, but you can endure and learn, can accept and be glad.

You will always come to the place where your *love* (your most abiding and intense thought) can receive its measure of gratification. If your love be base, you will come to a base place; if it be beautiful, you will come to a beautiful place.

You can alter your thoughts, and so alter your condition. Strive to perceive the vastness and grandeur of your responsibility. You are powerful, not powerless. You are as powerful to obey as you are to disobey; as strong to be pure as to be impure; as ready for wisdom as for ignorance. You can learn what you will, can remain as ignorant as you choose. If you love knowledge, you will obtain it; if you love wisdom, you will secure it; if you love purity, you will realize it. All things await your acceptance, and you choose by the thoughts which you entertain.

A man remains ignorant because he loves ignorance and chooses ignorant thoughts; a man becomes wise because he loves wisdom and chooses wise thoughts. No man is hindered by another; he is only hindered by himself. No man suffers because of another; he suffers only because of himself. By the Noble Gateway of Pure Thought, you can enter the highest Heaven; by the ignoble doorway of impure thought, you can descend into the lowest hell.

Your mental attitude towards others will faithfully react upon yourself and will manifest itself in every relation of your life. Every impure and selfish thought that you send out comes back to you in your circumstances in some form of suffering; every pure and unselfish thought returns to you in some form of blessedness. Your circumstances are *effects* of which the cause is inward and invisible. As the father-mother of your thoughts, you will perceive that every event in your life is weighed in the faultless balance of equity. When you understand the law within your mind, you will cease to regard yourself as the impotent and blind tool of circumstances and will become the strong and seeing master.

Note: This chapter originally printed as Chapter 10 in <u>Above Life's Turmoil</u>.

CHAPTER 3

Sowing and Reaping

There is a process of seed-sowing in the mind and life, a spiritual sowing which leads to a harvest according to the kind of seed sown. Thoughts, words, and acts are seeds sown, and, by the inviolable law of things, they produce after their kind.

Go into the fields and country lanes in the springtime, and you will see farmers and gardeners busy sowing seeds in the newly prepared soil. If you were to ask any one of those gardeners or farmers what kind of produce he expected from the seed he was sowing, he would doubtless regard you as foolish and would tell you that he does not "expect" at all, that it is a matter of common knowledge that his produce will be of the kind which he is sowing and that he is sowing wheat, or barley, or turnips, as the case may be, in order to reproduce that particular kind.

Every fact and process in Nature contains a moral lesson for the wise man. There is no law in the world of Nature around us which is not to be found operating with the same mathematical certainty in the mind of man and in human life. All the parables of Jesus are illustrative of this

truth and are drawn from the simple facts of Nature. There
is a process of seed-sowing in the mind and life, a spiritual
sowing which leads to a harvest according to the kind of
seed sown. Thoughts, words, and acts are seeds sown, and,
by the inviolable law of things, they produce after their
kind.

The man who thinks hateful thoughts brings hatred
upon himself. The man who thinks loving thoughts is
loved. The man whose thoughts, words, and acts are sincere is surrounded by sincere friends; the insincere man is
surrounded by insincere friends. The man who sows wrong
thoughts and deeds and prays that God will bless him is in
the position of a farmer who, having sown tares, asks God
to bring forth for him a harvest of wheat.

> "That which ye sow, ye reap;
>   See yonder fields —
>   The sesame was sesame, the corn was corn;
>   The silence and darkness knew;
>   So is a man's fate born.
>   He becometh reaper of the things he sowed."

He who would be blest, let him scatter blessings. He
who would be happy, let him consider the happiness of
others.

Then there is another side to this seed sowing. The
farmer must scatter all his seed upon the land and then
leave it to the elements. Were he to covetously hoard his
seed, he would lose both it and his produce for his seed
would perish. It perishes when he sows it, but in perishing
it brings forth a greater abundance. So in life, we get by
giving; we grow rich by scattering. The man who says he is

in possession of knowledge which he cannot give out because the world is incapable of receiving it either does not possess such knowledge, or, if he does, will soon be deprived of it — if he is not already so deprived. To hoard is to lose; to exclusively retain is to be dispossessed.

Even the man who would increase his material wealth must be willing to part with (invest) what little capital he has and then wait for the increase. So long as he retains his hold on his precious money, he will not only remain poor but will be growing poorer every day. He will, after all, lose the thing he loves and will lose it without increase. But if he wisely lets it go; if, like the farmer, he scatters his seeds of gold, then he can faithfully wait for, and reasonably expect, the increase.

Men are asking God to give them peace and purity and righteousness and blessedness but are not obtaining these things, and why not? Because they are not practicing them, not sowing them. I once heard a preacher pray very earnestly for forgiveness, and shortly afterwards, in the course of his sermon, he called upon his congregation to "show no mercy to the enemies of the church." Such self-delusion is pitiful, and men have yet to learn that the way to obtain peace and blessedness is to scatter peaceful and blessed thoughts, words, and deeds.

Men believe that they can sow the seeds of strife, impurity, and unbrotherliness, and then gather in a rich harvest of peace, purity, and accord by merely asking for it. What more pathetic sight than to see an irritable and quarrelsome man praying for peace. Men reap that which they sow, and any man can reap all blessedness now and at once if he will put aside selfishness and so broadcast the seeds of kindness, gentleness, and love.

If a man is troubled, perplexed, sorrowful, or unhappy, let him ask:

> "What mental seeds have I been sowing?"
> "What seeds *am* I sowing?"
> "What have I done for others?"
> "What is my attitude towards others?"
> "What seeds of trouble and sorrow and
> unhappiness have I sown that I should thus reap
> these bitter weeds?"

Let him seek within and find, and having found, let him
abandon all the seeds of self, and sow, henceforth, only the
seeds of Truth. Let him learn of the farmer the simple
truths of wisdom.

Note: This chapter originally printed as Chapter 11 in <u>Above Life's Turmoil</u>.

CHAPTER 4

Self-Discipline

*Before a man can accomplish anything of
an enduring nature in the world, he must
first of all acquire some measure of success
in the management of his own mind.*

A man does not *live* until he begins to discipline himself; he merely *exists*. Like an animal he gratifies his desires
and pursues his inclinations just where they may lead him.
He is happy as a beast is happy because he is not conscious
of what he is depriving himself. He suffers as the beast suffers because he does not know the way out of suffering.
He does not intelligently reflect upon life and lives in a
series of sensations, longings, and confused memories
which are unrelated to any central idea or principle. A man
whose inner life is so ungoverned and chaotic must neces-
sarily manifest this confusion in the visible conditions of
his outer life in the world; and though for a time, running
with the stream of his desires, he may draw to himself a
more or less large share of the outer necessities and com-
forts of life, he never achieves any real success nor ac-
complishes any real good, and sooner or later worldly
failure and disaster are inevitable as the direct result of

the inward failure to properly adjust and regulate those mental forces which make the outer life.

Before a man can accomplish anything of an enduring nature in the world, he must first of all acquire some measure of success in the management of his own mind. This is as mathematical a truism as that two and two are four, for "out of the heart are the issues of life." If a man cannot govern the forces within himself, he cannot long hold a firm hand upon the outer activities which form his visible life. On the other hand, as a man succeeds in governing himself, he rises to higher and higher levels of power and usefulness and success in the world.

The only difference between the life of the beast and that of the undisciplined man is that the man has a wider variety of desires and experiences a greater intensity of suffering. It may be said of such a man that he is dead, being truly dead to self-control, chastity, fortitude, and all the nobler qualities which constitute *life*. In the consciousness of such a man, the crucified Christ lies entombed, awaiting that resurrection which shall revivify the mortal suffering and wake him up to a knowledge of the realities of his existence.

With the practice of self-discipline, a man begins to live for he then commences to rise above the inward confusion and to adjust his conduct to a steadfast center within himself. He ceases to follow where inclination leads him, reins in the steed of his desires, and lives in accordance with the dictates of reason and wisdom. Hitherto his life has been without purpose or meaning, but now he begins to consciously mold his own destiny; he is "clothed and in his right mind."

In the process of self-discipline there are three stages, namely:

1. Control
2. Purification.
3. Relinquishment.

A man begins to discipline himself by controlling those passions which have hitherto controlled him; he resists temptations and guards himself against all those tendencies to selfish gratifications which are so easy and natural and which have formerly dominated him. He brings his appetite into subjection, and begins to eat as a reasonable and responsible being, practicing moderation and thoughtfulness in the selection of his food with the object of making his body a pure instrument through which he may live and act as becomes a man and no longer degrading that body by pandering to gustatory pleasure. He puts a check upon his tongue, his temper, and, in fact, his every animal desire and tendency, and this he does by referring all his acts to a fixed center within himself. It is a process of living from within outward, instead of, as formerly, from without inward. He conceives of an ideal, and, enshrining that ideal in the sacred recesses of his heart, he regulates his conduct in accordance with its exactions and demands.

There is a philosophical hypothesis that at the heart of every atom and every aggregation of atoms in the universe there is a *motionless center* which is the sustaining source of all the universal activities. Be this as it may, there is certainly in the heart of every man and woman a *selfless center* without which the outer man could not be, and which to ignore would lead to suffering and confusion. This selfless center which takes the form, in the mind, of an *ideal of unselfishness* and spotless purity, the attainment of which is desirable, is man's eternal refuge from the storms of passion and all the conflicting elements of his lower nature. It is the Rock of Ages, the Christ within, the divine and immortal in all men.

As a man practices self-control, he approximates more and more to this inward reality and is less and less swayed by passion and grief, pleasure and pain, and lives a steadfast and virtuous life, manifesting manly strength and fortitude. The restraining of the passions, however, is merely the initial stage in self-discipline and is immediately followed by the process of *Purification*. By this a man so purifies himself as to take passion out of the heart and mind altogether; not merely *restraining* it when it rises within him, but preventing it from rising altogether. By merely restraining his passions, a man can never arrive at peace, can never actualize his ideal; he must purify those passions.

It is in the purification of his lower nature that a man becomes strong and God-like, standing firmly upon the ideal center within, and rendering all temptations powerless and ineffectual. This purification is effected by thoughtful care, earnest meditation, and holy aspiration; and as success is achieved, confusion of mind and life pass away and calmness of mind and spiritualized conduct ensue.

True strength and power and usefulness are born of self-purification, for the lower animal forces are not lost but are transmuted into intellectual and spiritual energy. The pure life (pure in thought and deed) is a life of conservation of energy; the impure life (even should the impurity not extend beyond thought) is a life of dissipation of energy. The pure man is more capable, and therefore more fit, to succeed in his plans and to accomplish his purposes than the impure. Where the impure man fails, the pure man will step in and be victorious because he directs his energies with a calmer mind and a greater definiteness and strength of purpose.

With the growth in purity, all the elements which constitute a strong and virtuous manhood are developed in an increasing degree of power; and as a man brings his lower nature into subjection and makes his passions do his bidding, just so much will he mold the outer circumstances of his life, and influence others for good.

The third stage of self-discipline, that of *Relinquishment*, is a process of letting the lower desires and all impure and unworthy thoughts drop out of the mind and also refusing to give them any admittance, leaving them to perish. As a man grows purer, he perceives that all evil is powerless unless it receives his encouragement, and so he ignores it and lets it pass out of his life. It is by pursuing this aspect of self-discipline that a man enters into and realizes the divine life and manifests those qualities which are distinctly divine such as wisdom, patience, non-resistance, compassion, and love. It is here, also, where a man becomes consciously immortal, rising above all the fluctuations and uncertainties of life and living in an intelligent and unchangeable peace.

By self-discipline, a man attains to every degree of virtue and holiness and finally becomes a purified son of God, realizing his oneness with the central heart of all things.

Without self-discipline, a man drifts lower and lower, approximating more and more nearly to the beast, until at last he grovels, a lost creature, in the mire of his own befoulment. By self-discipline, a man rises higher and higher, approximating more and more nearly to the divine, until at last he stands erect in his divine dignity, a saved soul, glorified by the radiance of his purity. Let a man discipline himself, and he will live; let a man cease to discipline himself, and he will perish. As a tree grows in beauty, health, and fruitfulness by being carefully pruned and tended, so a man grows in grace and beauty of life by cutting away all the branches of evil from his mind and as he tends and develops the good by constant and unfailing effort.

As a man by practice acquires proficiency in his craft, so the earnest man acquires proficiency in goodness and wisdom. Men shrink from self-discipline because in its early stages it is painful and repellent, and the yielding to desire is, at first, sweet and inviting; but the end of desire is darkness and unrest, whereas the fruits of discipline are immortality and peace.

Note: This chapter originally printed as Chapter 15 in <u>Above Life's Turmoil</u>.

CHAPTER 5

Resolution

*For what is the real nature of resolution? Is
it not the sudden checking of a particular
stream of conduct, and the endeavor to
open up an entirely new channel?*

Resolution is the directing and compelling force in individual progress. Without it no substantial work can be
accomplished. Not until a man brings resolution to bear
upon his life does he consciously and rapidly develop; for
a life without resolution is a life without aims, and a life
without aims is a drifting and unstable thing.

Resolution may of course be linked to downward tendencies, but it is more usually the companion of noble
aims and lofty ideals, and I am dealing with it in this its
highest use and application.

When a man makes a resolution, it means that he is
dissatisfied with his condition and is commencing to take
himself in hand with a view to producing a better piece of
workmanship out of the mental materials of which his
character and life are composed; and insofar as he is true
to his resolution, he will succeed in accomplishing his purpose.

The vows of the saintly ones are holy resolutions directed toward some victory over self, and the beautiful achievements of holy men and the glorious conquests of the Divine Teachers were rendered possible and actual by the pursuit of unswerving resolution.

To arrive at the fixed determination to walk a higher path than heretofore, although it reveals the great difficulties which have to be surmounted, it yet makes possible the treading of that path and illuminates its dark places with the golden halo of success.

The true resolution is the crisis of long thought, protracted struggle, or fervent but unsatisfied aspiration. It is no light thing, no whimsical impulse or vague desire, but a solemn and irrevocable determination not to rest nor cease from effort until the high purpose which is held in view is fully accomplished.

Half-hearted and premature resolution is no resolution at all and is shattered at the first difficulty.

A man should be slow to form a resolution. He should searchingly examine his position and take into consideration every circumstance and difficulty connected with his decision and should be fully prepared to meet them. He should be sure that he completely understands the nature of his resolution, that his mind is finally made up, and that he is without fear and doubt in the matter. With the mind thus prepared, the resolution that is formed will not be departed from; and by the aid of it a man will, in due time, accomplish his strong purpose.

Hasty resolutions are futile. The mind must be fortified to endure.

Immediately as the resolution to walk a higher path is made, temptation and trial begin. Men have found that no sooner have they decided to lead a truer and nobler life than they have been overwhelmed with such a torrent of new temptations and difficulties as makes their position almost unendurable; and many men, because of this, relinquish their resolution.

But these temptations and trials are a necessary part of the work of regeneration upon which the man has decided, and must be hailed as friends and met with courage if the resolution is to do its work. For what is the real nature of resolution? Is it not the sudden checking of a particular stream of conduct, and the endeavor to open up an entirely new channel? Think of an engineer who decides to turn the course of a powerfully running stream or river in another direction. He must first cut his new channel and must take every precaution to avoid failure in the carrying out of his undertaking. But when he comes to the all-important task of directing the stream into its new channel, then the flowing force, which for ages has steadily pursued its accustomed course, becomes refractory, and all the patience and care and skill of the engineer will be required for the successful completion of the work. It is even so with the man who determines to turn his course of conduct in another and higher direction. Having prepared his mind, which is the cutting of a new channel, he then proceeds to the work of re-directing his mental forces — which have hitherto flowed on uninterruptedly — into the new course. Immediately as this is attempted, the arrested energy begins to assert itself in the form of powerful temptations and trials hitherto unknown and unencountered. And this is exactly as it should be; it is the law, and the same law that is in the water is in the mind. No man can improve upon the established law of things, but he can learn to understand the law instead of complaining and wishing things were different. The man who understands all that is involved in the regeneration of his mind will "glory in tribulations," knowing that only by passing through them can he gain strength, obtain purity of heart, and arrive at peace. And as the engineer at last (perhaps after many mistakes and failures) succeeds in getting the stream to flow on peacefully in the broader and better channel, and the turbulence of the water is spent, and all dams can be removed, so the man of resolution at last succeeds in directing his thoughts and acts into the better and nobler way to which he aspires, and temptations and trials give place to steadfast strength and settled peace.

He whose life is not in harmony with his conscience, and who is anxious to remedy his mind and conduct in a particular direction, let him first mature his purpose by earnest thought and self-examination, and having arrived at a final conclusion, let him frame his resolution, and having done so, let him not swerve from it, let him remain true to his decision under all circumstances, and he cannot fail to achieve his good purpose; for the Great Law ever shields and protects him who, no matter how deep his sins, or how great and many his failures and mistakes, has, deep in his heart, resolved upon the finding of a better way, and every obstacle must at last give way before a matured and unshaken resolution.

Note: This chapter originally printed as Chapter 16 in <u>Above Life's Turmoil</u>.

CHAPTER 6

Self-Control Leads to Happiness

*In speaking of self-control, one is easily
misunderstood. It should not be associated
with a destructive repression, but with a
constructive expression. The process is not
one of death, but of life;*

When mental energy is allowed to follow the line of
least resistance and to fall into easy channels, it is called
weakness; when it is gathered, focused, and forced into upward and difficult directions, it becomes power; and this
concentration of energy and acquisition of power is
brought about by means of self-control.

In speaking of self-control, one is easily
misunderstood. It should not be associated with a destructive repression, but with a constructive expression. The
process is not one of death, but of life; it is a divine and
masterly transmutation in which the weak is converted
into the strong, the coarse into the fine, and the base into
the noble; in which virtue takes the place of vice, and dark
passion is lost in bright intellectuality.

The man who merely smothers up and hides away his
real nature without any higher object in view than to create

a good impression upon others concerning his character is practicing hypocrisy and not self-control. As the mechanic transmutes coal into gas, and water into steam, and then concentrates and utilizes the finer forces thus generated for the comfort and convenience of men, so the man who intelligently practices self-control transmutes his lower inclinations into the finer qualities of intelligence and morality to the increase of his own and the world's happiness.

A man is happy, wise, and great in the measure that he controls himself; he is wretched, foolish, and mean in the measure that he allows his animal nature to dominate his thoughts and actions.

He who controls himself, controls his life, his circumstances, his destiny; and wherever he goes he carries his happiness with him as an abiding possession. He who does not control himself is controlled by his passions, by his circumstances, and by his fate; and if he cannot gratify the desire of the moment, he is disappointed and miserable. He depends for his fitful happiness on external things.

There is no force in the universe which can be annihilated or lost. Energy is transformed but not destroyed. To shut the door upon old and bad habits is to open it to new and better ones. Renunciation precedes regeneration. Every self-indulgence, every forbidden pleasure, every hateful thought renounced is transformed into something more purely and permanently beautiful. Where debilitating excitements are cut off, there spring up rejuvenating joys. The seed dies that the flower may appear; the grub perishes, but the dragon-fly comes forth.

Truly, the transformation is not instantaneous; nor is the transition a pleasant and painless process. Nature demands effort and patience as the price of growth. In the march of progress, every victory is contested with struggle and pain; but the victory is achieved, and it abides. The struggle passes; the pain is temporary only. To demolish a firmly fixed habit, to break up a mental tendency that has become automatic with long use, and to force into birth and growth a fine characteristic or lofty virtue — to accomplish this necessitates a painful metamorphosis, a transitional period of darkness, which to pass through patience and endurance are required; and this is where men fail. This is where they slip back into their old, easy, animal ruts and abandon self-control as too strenuous and severe. Thus they fall short of permanent happiness, and the life of triumph over evil is hidden from their eyes.

The permanent happiness which men seek in dissipation, excitement, and abandonment to unworthy pleasures is found only in the life which reverses all this — the life of self-control. So far as a man deviates from perfect self-command, just so far does he fall short of perfect happiness and sinks into misery and weakness, the lowest limit of which is madness, entire lack of mental control, the condition of irresponsibility. In so far as a man approximates to perfect self-command, just so near does he approach to perfect happiness and rises into joy and strength; and so glorious are the possibilities of such divine manhood that no limit can be set to its grandeur and bliss.

If a man will understand how intimately, yea, how inseparably, self-control and happiness are associated, he has but to look into his own heart, and upon the world around, to find there the joy destroying effects of uncontrolled tendencies. Looking upon the lives of men and women, he will perceive how the hasty word, the bitter retort, the act of deception, the blind prejudice and foolish resentment bring wretchedness and even ruin in their train. Looking into his own life, what days of consuming remorse, of restless anxiety, and of crushing sorrow rise up before his mind — periods of intense suffering through which he has passed through lack of self-control.

But in the right life, the well-governed life, the victorious life, all these things pass away. New conditions begin, and purer, more espiritual instruments are employed for the achievements of happy ends. There is no more remorse because there is no more wrong-doing; there is no more anxiety because there is no more selfishness; there is no more sorrow because Truth is the source of action.

That much-desired thing which self pursues with breathless and uncontrolled eagerness, yet fails to overtake, comes unbidden, and begs to be admitted, to him who works and waits in perfect self-command. Hatred, impatience, greed, self-indulgence, vain ambitions, and blind desires — the instruments by which self shapes its ill-finished existence, what clumsy tools they are, and how ignorant and unskillful are they who employ them! Love, patience, kindness, self-discipline, transmuted ambitions and chastened desires — instruments of Truth, by which is shaped a well-finished existence, what perfect tools they are, and how wise and skillful are they who use them!

Whatsoever is gained by feverish haste and selfish desire is attained in fuller measure by quietness and renunciation. Nature will not be hastened. She brings all to perfection in due season. Truth will not be commanded.

He has his conditions, and must be obeyed. Nothing is more superfluous than haste and anger. A man has to learn that he cannot command things, but that he can command himself; that he cannot coerce the wills of others, but that he can mold and master his own will: and things serve him who serves Truth; people seek guidance of him who is master of himself.

It is a little understood, yet simple and profound truth, that the man who cannot command himself under the severest external stress is unfit to guide others or to control affairs. It is the fundamental principle in the moral and political teaching of Confucius that, before attempting to govern affairs, a man should learn to govern himself. Men who habitually give way, under pressure, to hysterical suspicions, outbursts of resentment, and explosions of anger, are unfit for weighty responsibilities and lofty duties, and usually fail, sooner or later, even in the ordinary duties of life, such as the management of their own family or business. Lack of self-control is foolishness, and folly cannot take precedence over wisdom.

He who is learning how to subdue and control his turbulent, wandering thoughts is becoming wiser every day; and though for a time the Temple of Joy will not be completed, he will gather strength in laying its foundations and building up its walls; and the day will come when, like a wise master-builder, he will rest at peace in the beautiful habitation which he has built. Wisdom exists in self-control, and in wisdom is "pleasantness and peace."

The life of self-control is no barren deprivation, no wilderness of monotony. Renunciation there is, but it is the renunciation of the ephemeral and false in order that the abiding and true may be realized. Enjoyment is not cut off; it is intensified. Enjoyment is life; it is the slavish desire for it that kills. Is there anywhere a more miserable man than he who is always longing for some new sensation? Is there anywhere a more blessed being than he who, by self-control, is satisfied, calm, and enlightened? Who has most of physical life and joy—the glutton, the drunkard, and the sensualist who lives for pleasure only, or the temperate man who holds his body in subjection, considering its needs and obeying its uses? I was once eating a ripe, juicy apple as it came from the tree, and a man near me said, "I would give anything if I could enjoy an apple like that." I asked, "Why can't you?" His answer was, "I have drunk whisky and smoked tobacco until I have lost all enjoyment in such things." In pursuit of elusive enjoyments, men lose the abiding joys of life.

And as he who controls his senses has most of physical life, and joy, and strength, so he who controls his thoughts has most of spiritual life, and bliss, and power; for not only happiness, but knowledge and wisdom also are revealed by self-control. As the avenues of ignorance and selfishness are closed, the open gates of knowledge and enlightenment appear. Virtue attained is knowledge gained. The pure mind is the enlightened mind. He has well-being who controls himself well.

I hear men speak of the "monotony of goodness." If longing for things in the spirit which one has given up in the letter were "goodness," then it would indeed be monotonous. The man of self-control does not merely give up his base pleasures, he abandons all longing for them. He presses forward and does not look back; and fresh beauties, new glories, sublimer vistas await him at every step.

I am astonished at the revelations which lie hidden in self-control; I am captivated by the infinite variety of Truth; I am filled with joy at the grandeur of the prospect; I am gladdened by its splendor and its peace.

Along the way of self-control there is the joy of victory, the consciousness of expanding and increasing power, the acquisition of the imperishable riches of divine knowledge, and the abiding bliss of service to humankind. Even he who travels only a portion of the way will develop strength, achieve a success, and experience a joy which the idle and the thoughtless cannot know; and he who goes all the way will become a spiritual conqueror; he will triumph over all evil, and will blot it out; he will gaze with enrapt vision upon the majesty of the Cosmic Order and will enjoy the immortality of Truth.

Note: This chapter originally printed as Chapter 4 in <u>The Life Triumphant</u>.

CHAPTER 7

Right-Thinking and Repose

A man may be learned, but if he is not wise he will not be a true thinker. Not by learning will a man triumph over evil; not by much study will he overcome sin and sorrow. Only by conquering himself will he conquer evil; only by practicing righteousness will he put an end to sorrow.

Life is a combination of habits, some baneful, some beneficent, all of which take their rise in the one habit of thinking. The thought makes the man, therefore right-thinking is the most important thing in life. The essential difference between a wise man and a fool is that the wise man controls his thinking, the fool is controlled by it. A wise man determines how and what he shall think and does not allow external things to divert his thought from the main purpose; but a fool is carried captive by every tyrant thought that is aroused within him by external things, and he goes through life the helpless tool of impulse, whim, and passion.

Careless, slovenly thinking, commonly called thoughtlessness, is the companion of failure, wrong-doing, and wretchedness. Nothing, no prayers, no religious ceremonies, not even acts of charity, can make up for wrong-thinking. Only right-thinking can rectify a wrong life. Only the right attitude of mind towards men and things can bring repose and peace.

The Triumphant Life is only for him whose heart and intellect are attuned to lofty virtue. He must make his thought logical, sequential, harmonious, symmetrical. He must mold and shape his thinking to fixed principles and thereby establish his life on the sure foundation of knowledge. He must not merely be kind, he must be intelligently kind, must know why he is kind. His kindness must be an invariable quality and not an intermittent impulse interspersed with fits of resentment and acts of harshness. He must not merely be virtuous under virtuous circumstances; his virtue must be of that kind that shall continue to shine with unabated light when he is assailed with vicious circumstances. He must not allow himself to be hurled from the throne of divine manhood by the shocks of fate or the praise and blame of those about him. Virtue must be his abiding habitation, his refuge from the whirlwind and the storm.

And virtue is not only of the heart; it is of the intellect also; and without this virtue of the intellect, the virtue of the heart is imperiled. Reason, like passion, has its vices. Metaphysical speculations are the riot of the intellect as sensuality is the riot of the affections. The highest flights of speculation—pleasing as they are—reveal no place of rest, and the strained mind must return to facts and moral principles to find that truth which it seeks. As the soaring bird returns for refuge and rest to its nest in the rock, so must the speculative thinker return to the rock of virtue for surety and peace.

The intellect must be trained to comprehend the principles of virtue and to understand all that is involved in their practice. Its energies must be restrained from wasteful indulgence in vain subtleties and be directed in the path of righteousness and the way of wisdom. The thinker must distinguish, in his own mind, between reality and assumption. He must discover the extent of his actual knowledge. He must know what he knows. He must also know what he does not know. He must learn to discriminate between facts and opinions about facts, between belief and knowledge, error and Truth. In his search for the right attitude of mind which perceives truth, and works out a wise and radiant life, he must be more logical than logic, more merciless in exposing the errors of his own mind than the most sarcastic logician is in exposing the errors of the minds of others. After pursuing this course of discrimination for a short time, he will be astonished to find how small is the extent of his actual knowledge; yet he will be gladdened by its possession; for small as it is, it is the pure gold of knowledge; and what is better, to have a few grains of gold hidden away in tons of ore, where it is useless, or to extract the gold and throw away the ore? As the miner sifts away bushels of dull earth to find the sparkling diamond, so the spiritual miner, the true thinker, sifts away from his mind the accumulation of opinions, beliefs, speculations, and assumptions to find the bright jewel of Truth which bestows upon its possessor wisdom and enlightenment.

And the concentrated knowledge which is ultimately brought to light by this sifting process is found to be so closely akin to virtue that it cannot be divided from it, cannot be set apart as something different. In his search for knowledge, Socrates discovered virtue. The divine maxims of the Great Teachers are maxims of virtue. When knowledge is separated from virtue, wisdom is lost. What a man practices, that he knows. What he does not practice, that he does not know. A man may write treatises or preach sermons on love, but if he treat his family harshly, or think spitefully of his enemy, what knowledge has he concerning love? In the heart of the man of knowledge there dwells a silent and abiding compassion that shames the fine words of the noisy theorist. He only knows what peace is whose heart is free from hatred, who lives at peace with all. Cunning definitions of virtue only serve to deepen ignorance when they proceed from vice-stained lips. Knowledge has a deeper source than the mere memorizing of information. That knowledge is divine which proceeds from acquaintance with virtue. The humility which purges the intellect of its empty opinions and vain assumptions also fortifies it with a searching insight and invincible power. There is a divine logic which is indistinguished from love. The reply, "He that is without sin among you, let him first cast a stone at her," is unanswerable logic; it is also perfect love.

The wrong-thinker is known by his vices; the right-thinker is known by his virtues. Troubles and unrest assail the mind of the wrong-thinker, and he experiences no abiding repose. He imagines that others can injure, snub, cheat, degrade, and ruin him. Knowing nothing of the protection of virtue, he seeks the protection of self, and takes refuge in suspicion, spite, resentment, and retaliation, and is burnt in the fire of his own vices. When slandered, he slanders in return; when accused, he recriminates; when assailed, he turns upon his adversary with double fierceness. "I have been treated unjustly!" exclaims the wrong-thinker, and then abandons himself to resentment and misery. Having no insight, and unable to distinguish evil from good, he cannot see that it is his own evil, and not his neighbor's, that is the cause of all his trouble.

The right-thinker is not concerned with thoughts about self and self-protection, and the wrong actions of others towards him cannot cause him trouble or unrest. He cannot think — "This man has wronged me." He perceives that no wrong can reach him but by his own evil deeds. He understands that his welfare is in his own hands, and thus none but himself can rob him of repose. Virtue is his protection, and retaliation is foreign to him. He holds himself steadfastly in peace, and resentment cannot enter his heart. Temptation does not find him unprepared, and it assails in vain the strong citadel of his mind. Abiding in virtue, he abides in strength and peace.

The right-thinker has discovered and acquired the right attitude of mind toward men and things — the attitude of a profound and loving repose. And this is not resignation, it is wisdom. It is not indifference but watchful and penetrating insight. He has comprehended the facts of life; he sees things as they are. He does not overlook the particulars of life, but reads them in the light of cosmic law, sees them in their right relations as portions of the universal scheme. He sees that the universe is upheld by justice. He watches, but does not engage in, the petty quarrels and fleeting strifes of men. He cannot be a partisan. His sympathy is with all. He cannot favor one portion more than another. He knows that good will ultimately conquer in the world, as it has conquered in individuals; that there is a sense in which good already conquers, for evil defeats itself.

Good is not defeated; justice is not set aside. Whatever man may do, justice reigns; and its eternal throne cannot be assailed and threatened, much less conquered and overthrown; and this is the source of the true thinker's abiding repose. Having become righteous, he perceives the righteous law; having acquired evil, he knows that good is supreme.

He only is the true thinker whose heart is free from hatred, lust, and pride; who looks out upon the world through eyes washed free from evil; whose bitterest enemy arouses no enmity, but only tender pity in his heart; who does not talk vainly about things of which he has no knowledge and whose heart is always at peace.

And by this a man may know that his thoughts are in accordance with Truth-that there is no more bitterness in his heart, that malice has departed from him, that he loves where he formerly condemned.

A man may be learned, but if he is not wise he will not be a true thinker. Not by learning will a man triumph over evil; not by much study will he overcome sin and sorrow. Only by conquering himself will he conquer evil; only by practicing righteousness will he put an end to sorrow.

Not for the clever, nor the learned, nor the self-confident is the Life Triumphant, but for the pure, the virtuous, the wise. The former achieve their particular success in life, but the latter alone achieve the Great Success, a success so invincible and complete that even an apparent defeat shines with added victory.

Virtue cannot be shaken; virtue cannot be confounded; virtue cannot be overthrown. He who thinks in accordance with virtue, who acts righteously, whose mind is the servant of Truth, he it is who conquers in life and in death; for virtue must triumph, and Righteousness and Truth are the pillars of the universe.

Note: This chapter originally printed as Chapter 6 in <u>The Life Triumphant.</u>

CHAPTER 8

From Passion to Peace

Passion represents power, but power mis-directed, power producing hurt instead of happiness. It's forces, while being instruments of destruction in the hands of the foolish, are instruments of preservation in the hands of the wise. Passion is the flaming sword which guards the gates of Paradise. It shuts out and destroys the foolish; it admits and preserves the wise.

The pathway of the saints and sages; the road of the wise and pure; the highway along which the Saviours have trod, and which all Saviours to come will also walk — such is the subject of my writing; such is the high and holy theme which the author briefly expounds in these pages.

Passion is the lowest level of human life. None can descend lower. In its chilling swamps and concealing darkness creep and crawl the creatures of its sunless world. Lust, hatred, covetousness, pride, vanity, greed, revenge, envy, spite, retaliation, slander, backbiting, lying, theft, deceit, treachery, cruelty, suspicion, jealousy — such are the brute forces and blind, unreasoning impulses that inhabit the underworld of passion, and roam, devouring and devoured, in the rank primeval jungles of the human mind.

There also dwell the dark shapes of remorse and pain and suffering, and the drooping forms of grief and sorrow and lamentation.

In this dark world the unwise live and die, not knowing the peace of purity, nor the joy of that Divine Light which forever shines above them, and for them, yet shines in vain so long as it falls on unseeing eyes which look not up, but are ever bent earthward — fleshward.

But the wise look up. They are not satisfied with this passion-world, and they bend their steps towards the upper world of peace, the light and glory of which they behold, at first afar off, but nearer and with ever increasing splendor as they ascend.

None can fall lower than passion, but all can rise higher. In that lowest place where further descent is impossible, all who move forward must ascend; and the ascending pathway is always at hand, near, and easily accessible. It is the way of self-conquest, and he has already entered it who has begun to say "nay" to his selfishness, who has begun to discipline his desires, and to control and command the unruly elements of his mind.

Passion is the arch-enemy of mankind, the slayer of happiness, the opposite and enemy of peace. From it proceeds all that defiles and destroys. It is the source of suffering, the maker of misery, and the promulgator of mischief and disaster.

The inner world of selfishness is rooted in ignorance, — ignorance of Divine Law, of Divine Goodness; ignorance of the Pure Way and the Peaceful Path. Passion is dark, and it thrives and flourishes in spiritual darkness.

It cannot enter the regions of spiritual light. In the enlightened mind the darkness of ignorance is destroyed; in the pure heart there is no place for passion.

Passion in all its forms is a mental thirst, a fever, a torturing unrest. As a fire consumes a magnificent building, reducing it to a heap of unsightly ashes, so are men consumed by the flames of passions, and their deeds and works fall and perish.

If one would find peace, he must come out of passion. The wise man subdues his passions, the foolish man is subdued by them. The seeker for wisdom begins by turning his back on folly. The lover of peace enters the way which leads thereto, and with every step he takes he leaves further below and behind him the dark dwelling-place of passion and despair.

The first step towards the heights of wisdom and peace is to understand the darkness and misery of selfishness, and when that is understood, the overcoming it — the coming out of it — will follow.

Selfishness, or passion, not only subsists in the gross forms of greed and glaringly ungoverned conditions of mind; it forms also every hidden thought which is subtly connected with the assumption and glorification of one's self; and it is most deceiving and subtle when it prompts one to dwell upon the selfishness in others, to accuse them of it and to talk about it. The man who continually dwells upon the selfishness in others will not thus overcome his own selfishness. Not by accusing others do we come out of selfishness, but by purifying ourselves. The way from passion to peace is not by hurling painful charges against others, but by overcoming one's self. By eagerly striving to subdue the selfishness of others, we remain passion-bound; by patiently overcoming our own selfishness, we ascend into freedom. He only who has conquered himself can subdue others; and he subdues them, not by passion, but by love.

The foolish man accuses others and justifies himself; but he who is becoming wise justifies others and accuses himself. The way from passion to peace is not in the outer world of people; it is in the inner world of thoughts; it does not consist in altering the deeds of others, it consists in perfecting one's own deeds.

Frequently the man of passion is most eager to put others right; but the man of wisdom puts himself right. If one is anxious to reform the world, let him begin by reforming himself. The reformation of self does not end with the elimination of the sensual elements only; that is its beginning. It ends only when every vain thought and selfish aim is overcome. Short of perfect purity and wisdom, there is still some form of self-slavery or folly which needs to be conquered.

Passion is at the base of the structure of life; peace is its crown and summit. Without passion to begin with, there would be no power to work with, and no achievement to end with. Passion represents power, but power misdirected, power producing hurt instead of happiness. It's forces, while being instruments of destruction in the hands of the foolish, are instruments of preservation in the hands of the wise. When curbed and concentrated and beneficently directed, they represent working energy. Passion is the flaming sword which guards the gates of Paradise. It shuts out and destroys the foolish; it admits and preserves the wise.

He is the foolish man who does not know the extent of his own ignorance; who is the slave of thoughts of self; who obeys the impulses of passion. He is the wise man who knows his own ignorance; who understands the emptiness of selfish thoughts; who masters the impulses of passion.

The fool descends into deeper and deeper ignorance; the wise man ascends into higher and higher knowledge. The fool desires, and suffers, and dies. The wise man aspires, and rejoices, and lives.

With mind intent on wisdom, and mental gaze raised upward, the spiritual warrior perceives the upward way, and fixes his attention upon the heights of Peace.

Note: This chapter originally printed as chapter 1 in <u>From Passion to Peace.</u>

CHAPTER 9

Aspiration

Man attains in the measure that he aspires.
His longing to be is the gauge of what he
can be. To fix the mind is to foreordain the
achievment.

With the clear perception of one's own ignorance, comes the desire for enlightenment, and thus in the heart is born Aspiration, the rapture of the saints.

On the wings of aspiration man rises from earth to heaven, from ignorance to knowledge, from the under darkness to the upper light. Without it he remains a grovelling animal; earthly, sensual, unenlightened, and uninspired.

Aspiration is the longing for heavenly things — for righteousness, compassion, purity, love — as distinguished from desire, which is the longing for earthly things,-for selfish possessions, personal dominance, low pleasures, and sensual gratifications.

As a bird deprived of its wings cannot soar, so a man without aspiration cannot rise above his surroundings and become master of his animal inclinations. He is the slave of passions, is subject to others, and is carried hither and thither by the changing current of events.

For one to begin to aspire means that he is dissatisfied with his low estate, and is aiming at a higher condition. It is a sure sign that he is roused out of his lethargic sleep of animality, and has become conscious of nobler attainments and a fuller life.

Aspiration makes all things possible. It opens the way to advancement. Even the highest state of perfection conceivable it brings near and makes real and possible; for that which can be conceived can be achieved.

Aspiration is the twin angel to inspiration. It unlocks the gates of joy. Singing accompanies soaring. Music, poetry, prophecy, and all high and holy instruments, are at last placed in the hands of him whose aspirations flag not, whose spirit does not fail.

So long as animal conditions taste sweet to a man, he cannot aspire; he is so far satisfied; but when their sweetness turns to bitterness, then in his sorrow he thinks of nobler things. When he is deprived of earthly joy, he aspires to the joy which is heavenly. It is when impurity turns to suffering that purity is sought. Truly aspiration rises, phoenix-like, from the dead ashes of repentance, but on its powerful pinions man can reach the heaven of heavens.

The man of aspiration has entered the way which ends in peace; and surely he will reach that end if he stays not nor turns back. If he constantly renews his mind with glimpses of the heavenly vision, he will reach the heavenly state.

Man attains in the measure that he aspires. His longing to be is the gauge of what he can be. To fix the mind is to foreordain the achievment. As man can experience and know all low things, so he can experience and know all high things. As he has become human, so he can become divine. The turning of the mind in high and divine directions is the sole and needful task.

What is impurity but the impure thoughts of the thinker? What is purity but the pure thoughts of the thinker? One man does not do the thinking of another. Each man is pure or impure of himself alone.

If a man thinks, "It is through others, or circumstances, or heredity that I am impure," how can he hope to overcome his errors? Such a thought will check all holy aspirations, and bind him to the slavery of passion.

When a man fully perceives that his errors and impurities are his own, that they are generated and fostered by himself, that he alone is responsible for them, then he will aspire to overcome them, the way of attainment will be opened up to him, and he will see whence and whither he is travelling.

The man of passion sees no straight path before him, and behind him all is fog and gloom. He seizes the pleasure of the moment, and does not strive for understanding or think of wisdom. His way is confused, turbulent, troubled, and his heart is far from peace.

The man of aspiration sees before him the pathway up the heavenly heights, and behind him are the circuitous routes of passion up which he has hitherto blindly groped. Striving for understanding, and his mind set on wisdom, his way is clear, and his heart already experiences a foretaste of the final peace.

Men of passion strive mightily to achieve little things, — things which speedily perish, and, in the place where they were, leave nothing to be remembered.

Men of aspiration strive with equal might to achieve great things — things of virtue, of knowledge, of wisdom, which do not perish, but stand as monuments of inspiration for the uplifting of mankind.

As the merchant achieves worldly success by persistent exertion, so the saint achieves spiritual success by aspiration and endeavor. One becomes a merchant, the other a saint, by the particular direction in which his mental energy is guided.

When the rapture of aspiration touches the mind, it at once refines it, and the dross of its impurities begins to fall away; yea, while aspiration holds the mind, no impurity can enter it, for the impure and the pure cannot at the same moment occupy the thought. But the effort of aspiration is at first spasmodic and short-lived. The mind falls back into its habitual error, and must be constantly renewed.

The lover of the pure life renews his mind daily with the invigorating glow of aspiration. He rises early, and fortifies his mind with strong thoughts and strenuous endeavor. He knows that the mind is of such a nature that it cannot remain for a moment unoccupied, and that if it is not held and guided by high thoughts and pure aspirations, it will assuredly be enslaved and misguided by low thoughts and base desires.

Aspiration can be fed, fostered, and strengthened by daily habit, just as is desire. It can be sought, and admitted into the mind as a divine guide, or it can be neglected and shut out. To retire for a short time each day to some quiet spot, preferably in the open air, and there call up the energies of the mind in surging waves of holy rapture, is to prepare the mind for great spiritual victories and destinies of divine import; for such rapture is the preparation for wisdom and the prelude to peace. Before the mind can contemplate pure things it must be lifted up to them, it must rise above impure things; and aspiration is the instrument by which this is accomplished. By its aid the mind soars swiftly and surely into heavenly places, and begins to experience divine things; begins to accumulate wisdom, and to learn to guide itself by an ever increasing measure of the divine light of pure knowledge.

To thirst for righteousness; to hunger for the pure life; to rise in holy rapture on the wings of angelic aspiration — this is the right road to wisdom; this is the right striving for peace; this is the right beginning of the way divine.

Note: This chapter originally printed as Chapter 2 in <u>From Passion to Peace.</u>

CHAPTER 10

Temptation

*The stronghold of temptation is within a
man, not without; and until a man realizes
this, the period of temptation will be
protracted. When a man clearly perceives
that the evil is within, and not without, then
his progress will be rapid*

Aspiration can carry a man into heaven, but to remain
there he must learn to conform his entire mind to the
heavenly conditions: to this end temptation works.

Temptation is the reversion, in thought, from purity to
passion. It is a going back from aspiration to desire. It
threatens aspiration until the point is reached where
desire is quenched in the waters of pure knowledge and
calm thought. In the early stages of aspiration, temptation
is subtle and powerful, and is regarded as an enemy; but it
is only an enemy in the sense that the tempted one is his
own enemy. In the sense that it is the revealer of weakness
and impurity, it is a friend, a necessary factor in spiritual
training. It is, indeed, an accompaniment of the effort to
overcome evil and apprehend good. To be successfully
conquered, the evil in a man must come to the surface and

present itself, and it is in temptation that the evil hidden in the heart stands revealed and exposed.

That which temptation appeals to and arouses is un-conquered desire, and temptation will again and again as-sail and subdue a man until he has lifted himself above the lusting impulses. Temptation is an appeal to the impure. That which is pure cannot be subject to temptation.

Temptation waylays the man of aspiration until he touches the region of the divine consciousness, and beyond that border temptation cannot follow him. It is when a man begins to aspire that he begins to be tempted. Aspiration rouses up all the latent good and evil, in order that the man may be fully revealed to himself, for a man cannot overcome himself unless he fully knows himself. It can scarcely be said of the merely animal man that he is tempted, for the very presence of temptation means that there is a striving for a purer state. Animal desire and gratification is the normal condition of the man who has not yet risen into aspiration; he wishes for nothing more, nothing better, than his sensual enjoyments, and is, for the present, satisfied. Such a man cannot be tempted to fall, for he has not yet risen.

The presence of aspiration signifies that a man has taken one step, at least, upward, and is therefore capable of being drawn back, and this backward attraction is called temptation. The allurements of temptation subsist in the impure thoughts and downward desires of the heart. The object of temptation is powerless to attract when the heart no longer lusts for it. The stronghold of temptation is within a man, not without; and until a man realizes this, the period of temptation will be protracted. While a man continues to run away from outward objects, under the delusion that temptation subsists entirely in them, and does not attack and purge away his impure imaginings, his temptations will increase, and his falls will be many and grievous. When a man clearly perceives that the evil is within, and not without, then his progress will be rapid, his temptations will decrease, and the final overcoming of all temptation will be well within the range of his spiritual vision.

Temptation is torment. It is not an abiding condition, but is a passage from a lower condition to a higher. The fulness and perfection of life is bliss, not torment. Temptation accompanies weakness and defeat, but a man is destined for strength and victory. The presence of torment is the signal to rise and conquer. The man of persistent and ever renewed aspiration does not allow himself to think that temptation cannot be overcome. He is determined to be master of himself. Resignation to evil is an acknowledgment of defeat. It signifies that the battle against self is abandoned; that good is denied; that evil is made supreme.

As the energetic man of business is not daunted by difficulties, but studies how to overcome them, so the man of ceaseless aspiration is not crushed into submission by temptations, but meditates how he may fortify his mind; for the tempter is like a coward, he only creeps in at weak and unguarded points.

The tempted one should study thoughtfully the nature and meaning of temptation, for until it is known it cannot be overcome. A wise general, before attacking the opposing force, studies the tactics of his enemy; so he who is to overcome temptation must understand how it arises in his own darkness and error, and must study, by introspection and meditation, how to disperse the darkness and supplant error by truth.

The stronger a man's passions, the fiercer will be his temptations; the deeper his selfishness, the more subtle his temptations; the more pronounced his vanity, the more flattering and deceptive his temptations.

A man must know himself if he is to know truth. He must not shrink from any revelation which will expose his error; on the contrary, he must welcome such revelations as aids to that self-knowledge which is the handmaid of self-conquest.

The man who cannot endure to have his errors and shortcomings brought to the surface and made known, but tries to hide them, is unfit to walk the highway of truth. He is not properly equipped to battle with and overcome temptation. He who cannot fearlessly face his lower nature cannot climb the rugged heights of renunciation.

Let the tempted one know this: that he himself is both tempter and tempted; that all his enemies are within; that the flatterers which seduce, the taunts which stab, and the flames which burn, all spring from that inner region of ignorance and error in which he has hitherto lived; and knowing this, let him be assured of complete victory over evil. When he is sorely tempted, let him not mourn, therefore, but let him rejoice in that his strength is tried and his weakness exposed. For he who truly knows and humbly acknowledges his weakness will not be slow in setting about the acquisition of strength.

Foolish men blame others for their lapses and sins, but let the truth-lover blame only himself. Let him acknowledge his complete responsibility for his own conduct, and not say, when he falls, this thing, or such and such circumstance, or that man, was to blame; for the most which others can do is to afford an opportunity for our own good or evil to manifest itself; they cannot make us good or evil.

Temptation is at first sore, grievous, and hard to be borne, and subtle and persistent is the assailant; but if the tempted one is firm and courageous, and does not give way, he will gradually subdue his spiritual enemy, and will finally triumph in the knowledge of good....

Note: This chapter originally printed as Chapter 3 in From Passion to Peace.

CHAPTER 11

Transmutation

The enlightened man has abandoned the delusion that the evil in others has power to hurt and subdue him, and he has grasped the profound truth that he is only over-thrown by the evil in himself. He therefore ceases to blame others for his sins and suf-ferings and applies himself to purifying his own heart.

Midway between the hell of Passion and the heaven of Peace is the purgatory of Transmutation, — not a speculative purgatory beyond the grave, but a real purgatory in the human heart. In its separating and purifying fire the base metal of error is sifted away, and only the clarified gold of truth remains.

When temptation has culminated in sorrow and deep perplexity, then the tempted one, strenuously striving for deliverance, finds that his thraldom is entirely from himself, and that instead of fighting against outer circumstances, he must alter inner conditions. The fight against outer things is necessary at the commencement. It is the only course which can be adopted at the first, because of the prevailing ignorance of mental causation; but it never, of itself, brings about emancipation. What it does bring about is the knowledge of the mental cause of temptation; and the knowledge of the mental cause of temptation leads to the transmutation of thought, and the transmutation of thought leads to deliverance from the bondage of error.

The preliminary fighting is a necessary stage in spiritual development as the crying and kicking of a helpless babe is necessary to its growth; but as the crying and kicking is not needed beyond the infant stage, so the fierce struggling with, and falling under, temptation ends when the knowledge of mental transmutation is acquired.

The truly wise man, he who is enlightened concerning the source and cause of temptation, does not fight against outward allurements, he abandons all desire for them; they thus cease to be allurements, and the power of temptation is destroyed at its source. But this abandonment of unholy desire is not a final process, it is the beginning of a regenerative and transforming power which, patiently employed, leads man to the clear and cloudless heights of spiritual enlightenment.

Spiritual transmutation consists in an entire reversal of the ordinary self-seeking attitude of mind towards men and things, and this reversal brings about an entirely new set of experiences. Thus the desire for a certain pleasure is abandoned, cut off at its source, and not allowed to have any place in the consciousness; but the mental force which that desire represented is not annihilated, it is transferred to a higher region of thought, transmuted into a purer form of energy. The law of conservation of energy pertains as universally to mind as to matter, and the force shut off in lower directions is liberated in higher realms of spiritual activity.

Along the Saintly Way towards the divine life, the midway region of Transmutation is the Country of Sacrifice; it is the Plain of Renunciation. Old passions, old desires, old ambitions and thoughts are cast away and abandoned, but only to reappear in some more beautiful, more permanent, more eternally satisfying form. As valuable jewels, long guarded and cherished, are thrown tearfully into the melting-pot, yet are remolded into new and more perfect adornments, so the spiritual alchemist, at first loath to part company with long-cherished thoughts and habits, at last gives them up, to discover, a little later, to his joy, that they have come back to him in the form of new faculties, rarer powers, and purer joys—spiritual jewels newly burnished, beautiful and resplendent.

In transmuting his mind from evil to good, a man comes to distinguish more and more clearly between error and Truth, and so distinguishing, he ceases to be swayed and prompted by outward things, and by the actions and attitudes of others; he acts from his knowledge of truth. First acknowledging his errors, and then confronting them with a searching mind and a humble heart, he subdues, conquers, and transmutes them.

The early stage of transmutation is painful but brief, for the pain is soon transformed into pure spiritual joy, the brevity of the pain being measured by the intelligence and energy with which the process is pursued.

While a man thinks that the cause of his pain is in the attitude of others, he will not pass beyond it; but when he perceives that its cause is in himself, then he will pass beyond it into joy.

The unenlightened man allows himself to be disturbed, wounded, and overthrown by what he regards as the wrong attitude of others toward him; this is because the same wrong attitude is in himself. He, indeed, metes out to them, in return, the same actions, regarding as right in himself that which is wrong in others. Slander is given for slander, hatred for hatred, anger for anger. This is the action and reaction of evil; it is the clash of selfishness with selfishness. It is only the self, or selfish elements, within a man that can be aroused by the evil in another; the Truth, or divine characteristics, in a man cannot be approached by that evil, much less can it be disturbed and overthrown by it.

It is the conversion, or complete reversal, of this self into Truth that constitutes Transmutation. The enlightened man has abandoned the delusion that the evil in others has power to hurt and subdue him, and he has grasped the profound truth that he is only overthrown by the evil in himself. He therefore ceases to blame others for his sins and sufferings and applies himself to purifying his own heart. In this reversal of his mental attitude, he transmutes the lower selfish forces into the higher moral attributes. The base ore of error is cast into the fire of sacrifice, and there comes forth the pure gold of Truth.

Such a man stands firm and unmoved when assailed by outward things. He is self's master, not its slave. He has ceased to identify himself with the impulses of passion and has identified himself with Truth. He has overcome evil and has become merged in Good. He knows both error and Truth and has abandoned error and brought himself into harmony with Truth. He returns good for evil. The more he is assailed by evil from without, the greater is his opportunity of manifesting the good from within. That which supremely differentiates the fool from the wise man is this, — that the fool meets passion with passion, hatred with hatred, and returns evil for evil; whereas the wise man meets passion with peace, hatred with love, and returns good for evil.

Men inflict sufferings upon themselves through the active instrumentality of their own unpurified nature. They rise into perfect peace in the measure that they purify their hearts. The mental energy which men waste in the pursuance of dark passions is all-sufficient to enable them to reach the highest wisdom when it is turned in the right direction. As water, when transmuted into steam, becomes a new, more definite and wide-reaching power, so passion, when transmuted into intellectual and moral force, becomes a new life, a new power for the accomplishment of high and unfailing purposes.

Mental forces, like molecular, have their opposite poles or modes of action, and where the negative pole is, there also is the positive. Where ignorance is, wisdom is possible; where there is much suffering, much bliss is near. Sorrow is the negation of joy; sin is the opposite of purity; evil is the denial of good. Where there is an opposite, there is that which is opposed. The adverse evil, in its denial of the good, testifies to its presence. The one thing needful, therefore, is the turning round from the negative to the positive; the conversion of the heart from impure desires to pure aspirations; the transmutation of the passional forces into moral powers.

The wise purify their thoughts; they turn from bad deeds, and do good deeds; they put error behind them, and approach Truth. Thus do they rise above the allurements of sin, above the torments of temptation, above the dark world of sorrow, and enter the Divine Consciousness, the Transcendent Life.

Note: This chapter originally printed as Chapter 4 in <u>From Passion to Peace.</u>

CHAPTER 12

Heaven in the Heart

*In no outward place will the soul find
Heaven until it finds it within itself; for
wherever the soul goes its thoughts and
desires go with it; and however beautiful
may be its outward dwelling place, if there
is sin within, there will be darkness and
gloom without*

The toil of life ceases when the heart is pure. When the mind is harmonized with the Divine Law the wheel of drudgery ceases to turn, and all work is transmuted into joyful activity. The pure-hearted are as the lilies of the field, which toil not, yet are fed and clothed from the abundant storehouse of the All-Good. But the lily is not lethargic; it is ceaselessly active, drawing nourishment from earth and air and sun. By the Divine Power imminent within it, it builds itself up, cell by cell, opening itself to the light, growing and expanding toward the perfect flower. So is it with those who, having yielded up self-will, have learned to co-operate with the Divine Will. They grow in grace, goodness, and beauty, freed from anxiety, and without friction and toil. They never work in vain;

there is no wasted action. Every thought, act, and thing done subserves the Divine Purpose, and adds to the sum-total of the world's happiness.

Heaven is within. They will look for it in vain who look elsewhere. In no outward place will the soul find Heaven until it finds it within itself; for wherever the soul goes its thoughts and desires go with it; and however beautiful may be its outward dwelling place, if there is sin within, there will be darkness and gloom without; for sin casts a dark shadow over the pathway of the soul-the shadow of sorrow.

The world is beautiful, transcendently and wonderfully beautiful. Its beauties and inspiring wonders cannot be numbered; yet to the sin-sodden mind, it appears as a dark and joyless place. Where passion and self are, there is hell, and there are all the pains of hell; where Holiness and Love are, there is Heaven, and there are all the joys of Heaven.

Heaven is here. It is also everywhere. It is wherever there is a pure heart. The whole universe is abounding with joy, but the sin-bound heart can neither see, hear, nor partake of it. No one is, or can be, arbitrarily shut out from Heaven; each shuts himself out. Its Golden Gates are eternally ajar, but the selfish cannot find them; they mourn, yet see not; they cry, but hear not. Only to those who turn their eyes to heavenly things, their ears to heavenly sounds, are the happy Portals of the Kingdom revealed, and they enter and are glad.

All life is gladness when the heart is right, when it is attuned to the sweet chords of holy Love. Life is Religion, Religion is life, and all is Joy and Gladness. The jarring notes of creeds and parties, the black shadows of sin, let them pass away forever; they cannot enter the Door of Life; they form no part of Religion. Joy, Music, Beauty; these belong to the True Order of things; they are of the texture of the universe; of these is the divine Garment of Life woven. Pure Religion is glad, not gloomy. It is Light without darkness or shadow.

Despondency, disappointment, grief; these are the reflex aspects of pleasurable excitement, self-seeking, and desire. Give up the latter, and the former will always disappear; there remains the perfect Bliss of Heaven.

Abounding and unalloyed Happiness is man's true life; perfect Blessedness is his rightful portion; and when he loses his false life and finds the true he enters into the full possession of his Kingdom. The Kingdom of Heaven is man's Home; it is here and now, it is in his own heart, and he is not left without Guides if he wills to find it. All man's sorrows and suffering are the result of his own self-elected estrangement from the Divine Source, the All-Good, the Father, the Heart of Love. Let him return to his home; his peace awaits him.

The Heavenly-Minded are without sorrow and suffering because they are without sin. What the worldly-minded call troubles they regard as pleasant tasks of Love and Wisdom. Troubles belong to hell; they do not enter Heaven. This is so simple it should not appear strange. If you have a trouble it is in your own mind, and nowhere else; you make it, it is not made for you; it is not in your talk; it is not in that outward thing. You are its creator, and it derives its life from you only. Look upon all your difficulties as lessons to be learned, as aids to spiritual growth, and lo! they are difficulties no longer. This is one of the Pathways up to Heaven.

To transmute everything into Happiness and Joy, this is supremely the work and duty of the Heavenly-minded man. To reduce everything to wretchedness and deprivation is the process that the worldly-minded unconsciously pursue. To live in love is to work in Joy. Love is the magic that transforms all things into power and beauty. It brings plenty out of poverty, power out of weakness, loveliness out of deformity, sweetness out of bitterness, light out of darkness, and produces all blissful conditions out of its own substantial but indefinable essence.

He who loves can never want. The universe belongs to Goodness, and it therefore belongs to the good man. It can be possessed by all without stint or shrinking, for Goodness, and the abundance of Goodness — material, mental, and spiritual abundance — is inexhaustible. Think lovingly, speak lovingly, act lovingly, and every need shall be supplied; you shall not walk in desert places, and no danger shall overtake you.

Love sees with faultless vision, judges with true judgment, acts in wisdom. Look through the eyes of Love, and you shall see everywhere the Beautiful and the True; judge with the mind of love, and you shall err not, shall wake no wail of sorrow; act in the spirit of Love, and you shall strike eternal harmonies upon the Harp of Life.

Make no compromise with self. Cease not to strive until your whole being is swallowed up in Love. To love all and always; this is the Heaven of Heavens. "Let there be nothing within thee that is not very beautiful and very gentle, and then will there be nothing without thee that is not beautiful and softened by the spell of thy presence." All that you do, let it be done in calm wisdom and not from desire, impulse, or opinion; this is the Heavenly way of action.

Purify your thought-world until no stain is left, and you shall ascend into Heaven while living in the body. You will then see the things of the outward world clothed in all beautiful forms. Having found the Divine Beauty within ourselves, it springs to life in every outward thing. To the beautiful soul the world is beautiful.

Undeveloped souls are merely unopened flowers. The perfect Beauty lies concealed within and will one day reveal itself to the full-orbed light of Heaven. Seeing men thus, we stand where evil is not and where the eye beholds only good. Herein lies the peace and patience and beauty of Love: it sees no evil. He who loves thus becomes the protector of all men. Though in their ignorance they should hate him, he shields and loves them.

What gardener is so foolish as to condemn his flowers because they do not develop in a day? Learn to love, and you shall see in all souls, even those called degraded, the Divine Beauty, and shall know that it will not fail to come forth. This is one of the Heavenly Visions; it is out of this that Gladness comes.

Open the petals of your soul and let the glorious Light stream in.

Every soul is a resolved harmony. It shall at last strike the Perfect Chord and swell the joyful melodies of Heaven.

Hell is the preparation for Heaven; out of the debris of its ruined hovels are built pleasant mansions wherein the perfected soul may dwell.

Night is only a fleeting shadow which the world casts, and sorrow but a transient shade cast by the self. Come out into the Sunlight. Know this, O reader! that you are divine. You are not cut off from the Divine except in your own unbelief. Rise up, O Son of God! and shake off the nightmare of sin that binds you; accept your heritage: the Kingdom of Heaven! Drug your soul no longer with the poisons of false beliefs. You are not a worm of the dust unless you choose to make yourself one. You are a divine, immortal, God-born being, and this you may know if you will to seek and find. Cling no longer to your impure and grovelling thoughts, and you shall know that you are a radiant and celestial spirit, filled with all pure and lovable thoughts. Wretchedness and sin and sorrow are not your portion here unless you accept them as such; and if you do this, they shall be your portion hereafter, for these things are not apart from your soul-condition; they will go wherever you go; they are only within you.

Heaven, not hell, is your portion here and always. It only requires you to take what belongs to you. You are the master, and you choose whom you will serve. You are the maker of your state, and your choice determines your condition. What you pray and ask for — with your mind and heart, not with your lips merely — this you receive. You are served as you serve. You are conditioned as you condition. You garner in your own.

Heaven is yours; you have but to enter in and take possession; and Heaven means Supreme Happiness, Perfect Blessedness; it leaves nothing to be desired, nothing to be grieved over. It is complete satisfaction now and in this world. It is within you; and if you do not know this, it is because you persist in turning the back of your soul upon it. Turn around and you shall behold it.

Come and live in the sunshine of your being. Come out of the shadows and the dark places. You are framed for Happiness. You are a child of Heaven. Purity, Wisdom, Love, Plenty, Joy, and Peace: these are the eternal Realities of the Kingdom, and they are yours, but you cannot possess them in sin; they have no part in the realm of Darkness. They belong to "the Light which lighteth every man that cometh into the world," the Light of spotless Love. They are the heritage of the holy Christ-Child who shall come to birth in your soul when you are ready to divest yourself of all your impurities. They are your real self — your Divine Self.

Note: This chapter originally printed as Chapter 10 in The Heavenly Life.

CHAPTER 13

Mind Building and Life Building

*Character is built in the same way as a tree
or a house is built — namely, by the ceaseless addition of new material, and that
material is thought. By the aid of millions
of bricks, a city is built; by the aid of millions of thoughts, a mind, a character, is
built*

Everything both in nature and the works of man is
produced by a process of building. The rock is built up of
atoms; the plant, the animal, and man are built up of cells;
a house is built of bricks, and a book is built of letters. A
world is composed of a large number of forms, and a city
of a large number of houses. The arts, sciences, and institu-
tions of a nation are built up by the efforts of individuals.
The history of a nation is the building of its deeds.

The process of building necessitates the alternate
process of breaking down. Old forms that have served
their purpose are broken up, and the material of which
they are composed enters into new combinations. There
is reciprocal integration and disintegration. In all compounded bodies, old cells are ceaselessly being broken up,

and new cells are formed to take their place. The works of man also require to be continually renewed until they have become old and useless, when they are torn down in order that some better purpose may be served. These two processes of breaking down and building up in Nature are called death and life; in the artificial works of man they are called destruction and restoration.

This dual process, which pertains universally to things visible, also pertains universally to things invisible. As a body is built of cells, and a house of bricks, so a man's mind is built of thoughts. The various characters of men are none other than compounds of thoughts of varying combinations. Herein we see the deep truth of the saying, "As a man thinketh in his heart, so is he." Individual characteristics are fixed processes of thought; that is, they are fixed in the sense that they have become such an integral part of the character that they can be only altered or removed by a protracted effort of the will, and by much self-discipline. Character is built in the same way as a tree or a house is built — namely, by the ceaseless addition of new material, and that material is thought. By the aid of millions of bricks, a city is built; by the aid of millions of thoughts, a mind, a character, is built. "Rome was not built in a day," and a Buddha, a Plato, or a Shakespeare is not built in a lifetime.

Every man is a mind-builder, whether he recognizes it or not. Every man must perforce think, and every thought is another brick laid down in the edifice of mind. Such "brick-laying" is done loosely and carelessly by a vast number of people, the result being unstable and tottering characters that are ready to go down under the first little gust of trouble or temptation. Some, also, put into the building of their minds large numbers of impure thoughts; these are so many rotten bricks that crumble away as fast as they are put in, leaving always an unfinished and unsightly building, and one which can afford no comfort and no shelter for its possessor. Debilitating thoughts about one's health, enervating thoughts concerning unlawful pleasures, weakening thoughts of failure, and sickly thoughts of self-pity and self-praise are useless bricks with which no substantial mind-temple can be raised.

Pure thoughts, wisely chosen and well placed, are so many durable bricks which will never crumble away, and from which a finished and beautiful building, and one which affords comfort and shelter for its possessor, can be rapidly erected. Bracing thoughts of strength, of confidence, of duty; inspiring thoughts of a large, free, unfettered, and unselfish life, are useful bricks with which a substantial mind-temple can be raised; and the building of such a temple necessitates that old and useless habits of thought be broken down and destroyed.

"Build thee more stately mansions, O my soul! As the swift seasons roll."

Each man is the builder of himself. If he is the occupant of a jerry-built hovel of a mind that lets in the rains of many troubles, and through which blow the keen winds of oft-recurring disappointments, let him get to work to build a more noble mansion which will afford him better protection against those mental elements. Trying to weakly shift the responsibility for his jerry-building on to the devil, or his forefathers, or anything or anybody but himself, will neither add to his comfort, nor help him to build a better habitation.

When he wakes up to a sense of his responsibility, and an approximate estimate of his power, then he will commence to build like a true workman, and will produce a symmetrical and finished character that will endure, and be cherished by posterity, and which, while affording a never-failing protection for himself, will continue to give shelter to many a struggling one when he has passed away.

The whole visible universe is framed on a few mathematical principles. All the wonderful works of man in the material world have been brought about by the rigid observance of a few underlying principles; and all that there is to the making of a successful, happy, and beautiful life, is the knowledge and application of a few simple, root principles.

If a man is to erect a building that is to resist the fiercest storms, he must build it on a simple, mathematical principle, or law, such as the square or the circle; if he ignores this, his edifice will topple down even before it is finished.

Likewise, if a man is to build up a successful, strong, and exemplary life—a life that will stoutly resist the fiercest storms of adversity and temptation—it must be framed on a few simple, undeviating moral principles.

Four of these principles are—Justice, Rectitude, Sincerity, and Kindness. These four ethical truths are to the making of a life what the four lines of a square are to the building of a house. If a man ignores them and thinks to obtain success and happiness and peace by injustice, trickery, and selfishness, he is in the position of a builder who imagines he can build a strong and durable habitation while ignoring the relative arrangement of mathematical lines, and he will, in the end, obtain only disappointment and failure.

He may, for a time, make money, which will delude him into believing that injustice and dishonesty pay well; but in reality his life is so weak and unstable that it is ready at any moment to fall; and when a critical period comes, as come it must, his affairs, his reputation, and his riches crumble to ruins, and he is buried in his own desolation.

It is totally impossible for a man to achieve a truly successful and happy life who ignores the four moral principles enumerated, whilst the man who scrupulously observes them in all his dealings can no more fail of success and blessedness than the earth can fail of the light and warmth of the sun so long as it keeps to its lawful orbit; for he is working in harmony with the fundamental laws of the universe; he is building his life on a basis which cannot be altered or overthrown, and, therefore, all that he does will be so strong and durable, and all the parts of his life will be so coherent, harmonious, and firmly knit that it cannot possibly be brought to ruin.

In all the universal forms which are built up by the Great Invisible and unerring Power, it will be found that the observance of mathematical law is carried out with unfailing exactitude down to the most minute detail. The microscope reveals the fact that the infinitely small is as perfect as the infinitely great.

A snowflake is as perfect as a star. Likewise, in the erection of a building by man, the strictest attention must be paid to every detail.

A foundation must first be laid, and, although it is to be buried and hidden, it must receive the greatest care, and be made stronger than any other part of the building;

then stone upon stone, brick upon brick is carefully laid with the aid of the plum-line, until at last the building stands complete in its durability, strength, and beauty.

Even so it is with the life of a man. He who would have a life secure and blessed, a life freed from the miseries and failures to which so many fall victims, must carry the practice of the moral principles into every detail of his life, into every momentary duty and trivial transaction. In every little thing he must be thorough and honest, neglecting nothing.

To neglect or misapply any little detail—be he commercial man, agriculturist, professional man, or artisan—is the same as neglecting a stone or a brick in a building, and it will be a source of weakness and trouble.

The majority of those who fail and come to grief do so through neglecting the apparently insignificant details.

It is a common error to suppose that little things can be passed by, and that the greater things are more important, and should receive all attention; but a cursory glance at the universe, as well as a little serious reflection on life, will teach the lesson that nothing great can exist which is not made up of small details, and in the composition of which every detail is perfect.

He who adopts the four ethical principles as the law and base of his life, who raises the edifice of character upon them, who in his thoughts and words and actions does not wander from them, whose every duty and every passing transaction is performed in strict accordance with their exactions,— such a man, laying down the hidden foundation of integrity of heart securely and strongly, cannot fail to raise up a structure which shall bring him honor; and he is building a temple in which he can repose in peace

and blessedness — even the strong and beautiful Temple
of his life.

Note: This chapter originally printed In <u>The Mastery of Destiny.</u>

CHAPTER 14

The Cultivation of Concentration

*Scattered and diffused thoughts are weak
and worthless. Thoughts marshalled, commanded, and directed upon a given point,
are invincible; confusion, doubt, and difficulty give way before their masterly approach. Concentrated thought enters
largely into all successes, and informs all
victories.*

Concentration, or the bringing of the mind to a center
and keeping it there, is vitally necessary to the accomplishment of any task. It is the father of thoroughness and the
mother of excellence. As a faculty, it is not an end in itself,
but is an aid to all faculties, all work. Not a purpose in itself, it is yet a power which serves all purposes. Like steam
in mechanics, it is a dynamic force in the machinery of the
mind and the functions of life.

The faculty is a common possession, though in its perfection it is rare — just as will and reason are common possessions, though a perfectly poised will and a
comprehensive reason are rare possessions, — and the
mystery which some modern mystical writers have thrown

around it is entirely superfluous. Every successful man, in whatever direction his success may lie, practices concentration, though he may know nothing about it as a subject of study: every time one becomes absorbed in a book or task, or is rapt in devotion or assiduous in duty, concentration, in a greater or lesser degree, is brought into play.

Many books purporting to give instructions on concentration make its practice and acquisition an end in itself. Than this there is no surer nor swifter way to its destruction. The fixing of the eyes upon the tip of the nose, upon a door-knob, a picture, a mystical symbol, or the portrait of a saint; or the centering of the mind upon the navel, the pineal gland, or some imaginary point in space (I have seen all these methods seriously advised in works on this subject) with the object of acquiring concentration, is like trying to nourish the body by merely moving the jaw as in the act of eating, without taking food. Such methods prevent the end at which they aim. They lead towards dispersion and not concentration; towards weakness and imbecility rather than towards power and intelligence. I have met those who have squandered, by these practices, what measure of concentration they at first possessed, and have become the prey of a weak and wandering mind.

Concentration is an aid to the doing of something; it is not the doing of something in itself. A ladder has no value in and of itself, but only in so far as it enables us to reach something which we could not otherwise reach. In like manner, concentration is that which enables the mind to accomplish with ease that which it would be otherwise impossible to accomplish; but of itself it is a dead thing, and not a living accomplishment.

Concentration is so interwoven with the uses of life that it cannot be separated from duty; and he who tries to acquire it apart from his task, his duty, will not only fail, but will diminish, and not increase, his mental control and executive capacity, and so render himself less and less fit to succeed in his undertakings.

In the task of the hour is all the means for the cultivation of concentration — whether that task be the acquiring of divine knowledge, or the sweeping of a floor — without resorting to methods which have no practical bearing on life; for what is concentration but the bringing of a well-controlled mind to the doing of that which has to be done?

He who does his work in an aimless, a hurried, or thoughtless manner, and resorts to his artificial "Concentration methods" — to his door-knob, his picture, or nasal extremity — in order to gain that which he imagines to be some kind of mystical power — though he may drift towards insanity (and I knew one man who became insane by these practices), he will not increase in steadiness of mind.

The great enemy of concentration — and therefore of all skill and power — is a wavering, wandering, undisciplined mind; and it is in overcoming this that concentration is acquired. A scattered and undisciplined army would be useless. To make it effective in action and swift in victory it must be solidly concentrated and masterfully directed. Scattered and diffused thoughts are weak and worthless. Thoughts marshalled, commanded, and directed upon a given point, are invincible; confusion, doubt, and difficulty give way before their masterly approach. Concentrated thought enters largely into all successes, and informs all victories.

There is no more secret about its acquirement than about any other acquisition, for it is governed by the underlying principle of all development, namely, practice. To be able to do a thing, you must begin to do it, and keep on doing it until the thing is mastered.

This principle prevails universally — in all arts, sciences, trades; in all learning, conduct, religion. To be able to paint, one must paint; to know how to use a tool skillfully, he must use the tool; to become learned, he must learn; to become wise, he must do wise things; and to successfully concentrate his mind, he must concentrate it. But the doing is not all — it must be done with energy and intelligence.

The beginning of concentration, then, is to go to your daily task and put your mind on it, bringing all your intelligence and mental energy to a focus upon that which has to be done; and every time the thoughts are found wandering aimlessly away, they should be brought promptly back to the thing in hand. Thus the "center" upon which you are to bring your mind to a point, is not your pineal gland or a point in space, but the work which you are doing every day; and your object in thus concentrating is to be able to do your work with smooth rapidity and consummate skill; for until you can thus do your work, you have not gained any degree of control over the mind; you have not acquired the power of concentration.

This powerful focusing of one's thought and energy and will upon the doing of things is difficult at first — as everything worth acquiring is difficult — but daily efforts, strenuously made and patiently followed up, will soon lead to such a measure of self-control as will enable one to bring a strong and penetrating mind to bear upon any work undertaken; a mind that will quickly comprehend all the details of the work, and dispose of them with accuracy and despatch. He will thus, as his concentrative capacity increases, enlarge his usefulness in the scheme of things, and increase his value to the world, thus inviting nobler opportunities, and opening the door to higher duties; he will also experience the joy of a wider and fuller life.

In the process of concentration there are the four following stages:

1. Attention
2. Contemplation
3. Abstraction
4. Activity in Repose

At first the thoughts are arrested, and the mind is fixed upon the object of concentration, which is the task in hand — this is *attention*. The mind is then roused into vigorous thought concerning the way of proceeding with the task — this is *contemplation*. Protracted contemplation leads to a condition of mind in which the doors of the senses are all closed against the entrance of outside distractions, the thoughts being wrapped in, and solely and intensely centered upon, the work in hand — this is *abstraction*. The mind thus centered in profound cogitation reaches a state in which the maximum of work is accomplished with the minimum of friction — this is *activity in repose*.

Attention is the first stage in all successful work. They who lack it fail in everything. Such are the lazy, the thoughtless, the indifferent and incompetent. When attention is followed by an awakening of the mind to serious thought, then the second stage is reached. To ensure success in all ordinary, worldly undertakings, it is not necessary to go beyond these two stages. They are reached, in a greater or lesser degree, by all that large army of skilled and competent workers which carries out the work of the world in its manifold departents, and only a comparatively small number reach the third stage of *abstraction*; for when abstraction is reached, we have entered the sphere of genius. In the first two stages, the work and the mind are separate, and the work is done more or less laboriously, and with a degree of friction; but in the third stage, a marriage of the work with the mind takes place, there is a fusion, a union, and the two become one; then there is a superior efficiency with less labor and friction. In the perfection of the first two stages, the mind is objectively engaged, and is easily drawn from its center by external sights and sounds; but when the mind has attained perfection in abstraction, the *subjective* method of working is accomplished, as distinguished from the *objective*. The thinker is then oblivious to the outside world, but is vividly alive in his mental operations. If spoken to, he will not hear; and if plied with more vigorous appeals, he will bring back his mind to outside things as one coming out of a dream; indeed, this abstraction is a kind of waking dream, but its similarity to a dream ends with the subjective state; it does not pertain to the mental operations of that state, in which, instead of the confusion of dreaming, there is perfect order, penetrating insight, and a wide range of comprehension. Whoever attains perfection in abstraction will manifest genius in the particular work upon which his mind is centered. Inventors, artists, poets, scientists, philosophers, and all men of genius, are men of abstraction. They accomplish subjectively, and with ease, that which the objective workers — men who have not yet attained beyond the second stage in concentration — cannot accomplish with the most strenuous labor.

When the fourth state-that of *activity in repose* — is attained, then concentration in its perfection is acquired. I am unable to find a single word which will fully express this dual condition of intense activity combined with steadiness, or rest, and have therefore employed the term "activity in repose." The term appears contradictory, but the simple illustration of a spinning top will serve to explain the paradox. When a top spins at the maximum velocity, the friction is reduced to the minimum, and the top assumes that condition of perfect repose which is a sight so beautiful to the eye, and so captivating to the mind, of the schoolboy, who then says his top is "asleep." The top is apparently motionless, but it is the rest, not of inertia, but of intense and perfectly balanced activity. So the mind that has acquired perfect concentration is, when engaged in that intense activity of thought which results in productive work of the highest kind, in a state of quiet poise and calm repose. Externally, there is no apparent activity, no disturbance, and the face of a man who has acquired this power will assume a more or less radiant calmness, and the face will be more sublimely calm when the mind is most intensely engaged in active thought.

Each stage of concentration has its particular power. Thus the first stage, when perfected, leads to usefulness; the second leads to skill, ability, talent; the third leads to originality and genius; while the fourth leads to mastery and power, and makes leaders and teachers of men.

In the development of concentration, also, as in all objects of growth, the following stages embody the preceding ones in their entirety. Thus in contemplation, attention is contained; in abstraction, both attention and contemplation are embodied; and he who has reached the last stage, brings into play, in the act of contemplation, all the four stages.

He who has perfected himself in concentration is able, at any moment, to bring his thoughts to a point upon any matter, and to search into it with the strong light of an active comprehension. He can both take a thing up and lay it down with equal deliberation. He has learned how to use his thinking faculties to fixed purposes, and guide them toward definite ends. He is an intelligent doer of things, and not a weak wanderer amid chaotic thought.

Decision, energy, alertness, as well as deliberation, judgment, and gravity, accompany the habit of concentration; and that vigorous mental training which its cultivation involves, leads, through ever-increasing usefulness and success in worldly occupations, towards that higher form of concentration called "meditation," in which the mind becomes divinely illuminated and acquires the heavenly knowledge.

Note: This chapter originally printed in The Mastery of Destiny.

CHAPTER 15

The Practice of Meditation

*Man is a thought-being, and his life and
character are determined by the thoughts in
which he habitually dwells. By practice, association, and habit, thoughts tend to
repeat themselves with greater and greater
ease and frequency, and so "fix" the character in a given direction by producing that
automatic action which is called "habit."*

When *aspiration* is united to *concentration*, the result
is *meditation*. When a man intensely desires to reach and
realize a higher, purer, and more radiant life than the
merely worldly and pleasure loving life, he engages in
aspiration; and when he earnestly concentrates his
thoughts upon the finding of that life, he practices meditation.

Without intense aspiration, there can be no meditation. Lethargy and indifference are fatal to its practice.
The more intense the nature of a man, the more readily
will he find meditation, and the more successfully will he
practice it. A fiery nature will most rapidly scale the

heights of Truth in meditation, when its aspirations have become sufficiently awakened.

Concentration is necessary to worldly success; meditation is necessary to spiritual success. Worldly skill and knowledge are acquired by concentration: spiritual skill and knowledge are acquired by meditation. By concentration a man can scale the highest heights of genius, but he cannot scale the heavenly heights of Truth: to accomplish this, he must meditate. By concentration a man may acquire the wonderful comprehension and vast power of a Caesar; by meditation he may reach the divine wisdom and perfect peace of a Buddha. The perfection of concentration is *power*; the perfection of meditation is *wisdom*. By concentration, men acquire skill in the doing of the things of life — in science, art, trade, etc., — but by meditation, they acquire skill in *life* itself; in right living, enlightenment, wisdom, etc. Saints, sages, saviours — wise men and divine teachers-are the finished products of holy meditation.

The four stages in concentration are brought into play in meditation; the difference between the two powers being one of *direction*, and not of nature. Meditation is therefore *spiritual concentration*; the bringing of the mind to a focus in its search for the divine knowledge, the divine life; the intense dwelling, in thought, on Truth. Thus a man aspires to know and realize, above all things else, the Truth; he then gives *attention* to conduct, to life, to self-purification; giving attention to these things, he passes into serious *contemplation* of the facts, problems, and mystery of life: thus contemplating, he comes to love Truth so fully and intensely as to become wholly absorbed in it, the mind is drawn away from its wanderings in a multitude of desires, and, solving one by one the problems of life, realizes that profound union with Truth which is the state of *abstraction*; and thus absorbed in Truth, there is that balance and poise of character, that divine *action in repose*, which is the abiding calm and peace of an emancipated and enlightened mind.

Meditation is more difficult to practice than concentration because it involves a much more severe self-discipline than that which pertains to concentration. A man can practice concentration without purifying his heart and life, whereas the process of purification is inseparable from meditation. The object of meditation is divine enlightenment, the attainment of Truth, and is therefore interwoven with practical purity and righteousness. Thus while, at first, the time spent in actual meditation is short — perhaps only half an hour in the early morning — the knowledge gained in that half-hour of vivid aspiration and concentrated thought is embodied in practice during the whole day. In meditation, therefore, the entire life of a man is involved; and as he advances in its practice he becomes more and more fitted to perform the duties of life in the circumstances in which he may be placed, for he becomes stronger, holier, calmer, and wiser.

The principle of meditation is two-fold, namely:

> 1.Purification of the heart by repetitive thought on pure things.
> 2.Attainment of divine knowledge by embodying such purity in practical life.

Man is a *thought-being*, and his life and character are determined by the thoughts in which he habitually dwells.

By practice, association, and habit, thoughts tend to repeat themselves with greater and greater ease and frequency, and so "fix" the character in a given direction by producing that automatic action which is called "habit." By daily dwelling upon pure thoughts, the man of meditation forms the habit of pure and enlightened thinking which leads to pure and enlightened actions and well-performed duties. By the ceaseless repetition of pure thoughts, he at last becomes one with those thoughts, and is a purified being, manifesting his attainment in pure actions, in a serene and wise life.

The majority of men live in a series of conflicting desires, passions, emotions, and speculations, and there are restlessness, uncertainty, and sorrow; but when a man begins to train his mind in meditation, he gradually gains control over this inward conflict by bringing his thoughts to a focus upon a central principle. In this way the old habits of impure and erroneous thought and action are broken up, and the new habits of pure and enlightened thought and action are formed; the man becomes more and more reconciled to Truth, and there is increasing harmony and insight, a growing perfection and peace.

A powerful and lofty aspiration towards Truth is always accompanied with a keen sense of the sorrow and brevity and mystery of life, and until this condition of mind is reached, meditation is impossible. Merely musing, or whiling away the time in idle dreaming (habits to which the word meditation is frequently applied), are very far removed from meditation, in the lofty spiritual sense which we attach to that condition.

It is easy to mistake *reverie* for meditation. This is a fatal error which must be avoided by one striving to meditate. The two must not be confounded. Reverie is a loose dreaming into which a man falls; meditation is a strong, purposeful thinking into which a man rises. Reverie is easy and pleasurable; meditation is at first difficult and irksome. Reverie thrives in indolence and luxury; meditation arises from strenuousness and discipline. Reverie is first alluring, then sensuous, and then sensual. Meditation is first forbidding, then profitable, and then peaceful. Reverie is dangerous; it undermines self-control. Meditation is protective; it establishes self-control.

There are certain signs by which one can know whether he is engaging in reverie or meditation. The indications of reverie are:

1. A desire to avoid exertion.
2. A desire to experience the pleasures of dreaming.
3. An increasing distaste for one's worldly duties.
4. A desire to shirk one's worldly responsibilities.
5. Fear of consequences.
6. A wish to get money with as little effort as possible.
7. Lack of self-control.

The indications of meditation are:

1. Increase of both physical and mental energy.
2. A strenuous striving after wisdom.
3. A decrease of irksomeness in the performance of duty.
4. A fixed determination to faithfully fulfill all worldly responsibilities.

5.Freedom from fear.
6.Indifference to riches.
7.Possession of self-control.

There are certain times, places, and conditions in and under which it is impossible to meditate, others wherein it is difficult to meditate, and others wherein meditation is rendered more accessible; and these, which should be known and carefully observed, are as follows:

Times, Places, and Conditions in which Meditation is Impossible:

1.At, or immediately after, meals.
2.In places of pleasure.
3.In crowded places.
4.While walking rapidly.
5.While lying in bed in the morning.
6.While smoking.
7.While lying on a couch or bed for physical or
   mental relaxation.

Times, Places, and Conditions in which Meditation is Difficult.

1.At night.
2.In a luxuriously furnished room.
3.While sitting on a soft, yielding seat.
4.While wearing gay clothing.
5.When in company.
6.When the body is weary.
7.If the body is given too much food.

Times, Places, and Conditions in which it is Best to Meditate.

    1.Very early in the morning.
    2.Immediately before meals.
    3.In solitude.
    4.In the open air or in a plainly furnished room.
    5.While sitting on a hard seat.
    6.When the body is strong and vigorous.
    7.When the body is modestly and plainly clothed.

It will be seen by the foregoing instructions that ease, luxury, and indulgence (which induce reverie) render meditation difficult, and when strongly pronounced make it impossible; while strenuousness, discipline, and self-denial (which dispel reverie), make meditation comparatively easy. The body, too, should be neither over fed nor starved; neither in rags nor flauntingly clothed. It should not be tired, but should be at its highest point of energy and strength, as the holding of the mind to a concentrated train of subtle and lofty thought requires a high degree of both physical and mental energy.

Aspiration can often best be aroused, and the mind renewed in meditation, by the mental repetition of a lofty precept, a beautiful sentence or a verse of poetry. Indeed, the mind that is ready for meditation will instinctively adopt this practice. Mere mechanical repetition is worthless, and even a hindrance. The words repeated must be so applicable to one's own condition that they are dwelt upon lovingly and with concentrated devotion. In this way aspiration and concentration harmoniously combine to produce, without undue strain, the state of meditation.

All the conditions above stated are of the utmost importance in the early stages of meditation, and should be carefully noted and duly observed by all who are striving to acquire the practice; and those who faithfully follow the instructions, and who strive and persevere, will not fail to gather in, in due season, the harvest of purity, wisdom, bliss, and peace; and will surely eat of the sweet fruits of holy meditation.

Note: This chapter originally printed in the Mastery of Destiny.

CHAPTER 16

The Heart and the Life

*Let a man realize that life in its totality
proceeds from the mind, and lo, the way of
blessedness is opened up to him*

As is the heart, so is the life. The within is ceaselessly becoming the without. Nothing remains unrevealed. That which is hidden is but for a time; it ripens and comes forth at last. Seed, tree, blossom, and fruit is the four fold order of the universe. From the state of a man's heart proceed the conditions of his life; his thoughts blossom into deeds, and his deeds bear the fruitage of character and destiny.

Life is ever unfolding from within, and revealing itself to the light, and thoughts engendered in the heart at last reveal themselves in words, actions, and things accomplished.

As the fountain from the hidden spring, so issues man's life from the secret recesses of his heart. All that he is and does is generated there. All that he will be and do will take its rise there.

Sorrow and gladness, suffering and enjoyment, hope and fear, hatred and love, ignorance and enlightenment, are nowhere but in the heart; they are solely mental conditions.

Man is the keeper of his heart; the watcher of his mind; the solitary sentinel of his citadel of life. As such, he can be diligent or negligent. He can keep his heart more and more carefully; he can more strenuously watch and purify his mind; and he can guard himself against the thinking of unrighteous thoughts; this is the way of enlightenment and bliss. On the other hand, he can live loosely and carelessly, neglecting the supreme task of rightly ordering his life: this is the way of self-delusion and suffering.

Let a man realize that life in its totality proceeds from the mind, and lo, the way of blessedness is opened up to him! For he will then discover that he possesses the power to rule his mind, and to fashion it in accordance with his ideal. So will he elect to strongly and steadfastly walk those pathways of thought and action which are altogether excellent; to him life will become beautiful and sacred; and, sooner or later, he will put to flight all evil, confusion, and suffering; for it is impossible for a man to fall short of liberation, enlightenment, and peace, who guards with unwearying diligence the gateway of his heart.

Note: This chapter originally printed in <u>Out From the Heart.</u>

CHAPTER 17

The Nature and Power of Mind

The bonds of habit, impotence, and sin are self-made, and can only be destroyed by one's self; they exist nowhere but in one's mind, and although they are directly related to outward things, they have no real existence in those things

Mind is the arbiter of life; it is the creator and shaper of conditions, and the recipient of its own results. It contains within itself both the power to create illusion and to perceive reality.

Mind is the infallible weaver of destiny; thought is the thread, good and evil deeds are the warp of woof, and the web, woven upon the loom of life, is character. Mind clothes itself in garments of its own making.

Man, as a mental being possesses all the powers of mind, and is furnished with unlimited choice. He learns by experience, and he can accelerate or retard his experience. He is not arbitrarily bound at any point, but he has bound himself at many points, and having bound himself he can, when he chooses, liberate himself. He can become bestial or pure, ignoble or noble, foolish or wise, just as he chooses. He can, by recurring practice, form habits, and he can, by renewed effort, break them off. He can surround himself with illusions until Truth is completely lost, and he can destroy one and another of those illusions until Truth is entirely recovered. His possibilities are limitless; his freedom is complete.

It is in the nature of mind to create its own conditions, and to choose the states in which it shall dwell. It also has the power to alter any condition and to abandon any state, and this it is continually doing as it gathers knowledge of state after state by repeated choice and exhaustive experience.

Inward processes of thought make up the sum of character and life, and man can modify and alter these processes by bringing will and effort to bear upon them. The bonds of habit, impotence, and sin are self-made, and can only be destroyed by one's self; they exist nowhere but in one's mind, and although they are directly related to outward things, they have no real existence in those things. The outer is molded and vivified by the inner, and never the inner by the outer. Temptation does not arise in the outer object, but *in the lust of the mind for that object*; nor do suffering and sorrow inhere in the external things and happenings of life, but in an undisciplined attitude of mind toward those things and happenings. The mind that is disciplined by Purity and fortified by Wisdom, avoids all those lusts and desires which are inseparably bound up with affliction, and so arrives at enlightenment and peace.

To condemn others as evil, and to rail against outside conditions as the source of evil, increases, and does not lessen, the world's suffering and unrest. The outer is but the shadow and effect of the inner, and when the heart is pure all outward things are pure.

All growth and life is from within outward; all decay and death is from without inward; this is a universal law. All evolution proceeds from within. All adjustment must take place within. He who ceases to strive against others, and employs his powers in the transformation, regeneration, and development of his own mind, conserves his energies and preserves himself; and as he succeeds in harmonizing his own mind, he leads others by consideration and charity into a like blessed state, for not by assuming authority and guidance over other minds is the way of enlightenment and peace discovered, but by exercising a lawful authority over one's own and by guiding one's self in pathways of steadfast and lofty virtue.

A man's life proceeds from his heart, his mind; he has compounded that mind by his own thoughts and deeds; it is in his power to refashion that mind by his choice of thought; he can therefore transform his life.

Note: This chapter originally printed in Out From the Heart.

CHAPTER 18

The Formation of Habit

Just as an artisan becomes, by practice, accomplished in his craft, so a man can become, by practice, accomplished in goodness; it is entirely a matter of forming new habits of thought

Every established mental condition is *an acquired habit*, and it has become such by continuous repetition of thought. Despondency and cheerfulness, anger and calmness, covetousness and generosity—indeed, all states of mind—are habits built up by choice, until they have become automatic. A thought constantly repeated at last becomes a fixed habit of the mind, and from such habits proceeds the life.

It is in the nature of the mind to acquire knowledge by the repetition of its experiences. A thought which it is very difficult, at first, to hold and to dwell upon, at last becomes, by constantly being held in the mind, a natural and habitual condition. Just as a boy, when commencing to learn a trade, cannot even handle his tools aright, much less use them correctly, but after long repetition and practice plies them with perfect ease and consummate skill, so

a state of mind, at first apparently impossible of realization, is, by perseverance and practice, at last acquired and
built into the character as a natural and spontaneous condition.

In this power of the mind to form and reform its habits,
its conditions, is contained the basis of man's salvation,
and the open door to perfect liberty by the mastery of self,
for as a man has the power to form harmful habits, so he
has the same power to create habits that are essentially
good. And here we come to a point which needs some
elucidating, and which calls for deep and earnest thought
on the part of my reader.

It is commonly said to be easier to do wrong than right,
to sin than to be holy; such condition has come to be
regarded, almost universally, as axiomatic, and no less a
teacher than the Buddha has said: — "Bad deeds, and deeds
hurtful to ourselves, are easy to do; what is beneficial and
good, that is very difficult to do," — and as regards
humanity generally, this is true, but it is only true as a passing experience, a fleeting factor in human evolution; it is
not a fixed condition of things, is not of the nature of an
eternal truth. It is easier for men to do wrong than right,
because of the prevalence of *ignorance*, because the true
nature of things, and the essence and meaning of life, are
not apprehended. When a child is learning to write, it is
extremely easy for it to hold the pen wrongly, and to form
its letters incorrectly, but it is painfully difficult to hold the
pen and to write properly; and this because of the child's
ignorance of the art of writing, which can only be dispelled
by persistent effort and practice, until at last, it becomes
natural and easy to hold the pen properly, and to write correctly, and difficult, as well as altogether unnecessary, to

do the wrong thing. It is the same in the vital things of mind and life. To think and do rightly requires much practice and renewed effort, but the time at last comes when it becomes habitual and easy to think and do rightly, and difficult, as it is then seen to be altogether unnecessary, to do that which is wrong.

Just as an artisan becomes, by practice, accomplished in his craft, so a man can become, by practice, accomplished in goodness; it is entirely a matter of forming new habits of thought, and he to whom right thoughts have become easy and natural, and wrong thoughts and acts difficult to do, has attained to the highest virtue, to pure, spiritual knowledge.

It is easy and natural for men to sin, because they have formed by incessant repetition, harmful and unenlightened habits of thought. It is very difficult for the thief to refrain from stealing when opportunity occurs, because he has lived so long in covetous and avaricious thoughts; but such difficulty does not exist for the honest man who has lived so long in upright and honest thoughts, and has thereby become enlightened as to the wrong, folly, and fruitlessness of theft, that even the remotest idea of stealing does not enter his mind. The sin of theft is a very extreme one, and I have introduced it in order to the more clearly illustrate the force and formation of habit; but all sins and virtues are formed in the same way. Anger and impatience are natural and easy to thousands of people, because they are constantly repeating the angry and impatient thought and act, and with each repetition the habit is more firmly established and more deeply rooted. Calmness and patience can become habitual in the same way — by first grasping, through effort, a calm and patient thought, and then continuously thinking it, and living in it, until "use becomes second nature," and anger and impatience pass away forever. It is thus that every wrong thought may be expelled from the mind, thus that every untrue act may be destroyed; thus that every sin may be overcome.

Note: This chapter originally printed in <u>Out From the Heart.</u>

CHAPTER 19

On Doing and Knowing

Virtue can only be known by doing, and the knowledge of Truth can only be arrived at by perfecting one's self in the practice of Virtue and to be complete in the practice and acquisition of Virtue is to be complete in the knowledge of Truth.

Let a man realize that his life, in its totality, proceeds from his mind, and that his mind is a combination of habits which he can, by patient effort, modify to any extent, and over which he can thus gain complete ascendency and control, and he has at once obtained possession of the key which shall open the door to his complete emancipation.

But emancipation from the ills of life (which are the ills of one's mind) is a matter of steady growth from within, and not a sudden acquisition from without. Hourly and daily must the mind be trained to think stainless thoughts, and to adopt right and dispassionate attitudes under those circumstances in which it is prone to fall into wrong and passion. Like the patient sculptor upon his marble, the aspirant to the Right Life must gradually work upon the

crude material of his mind until he has wrought out of it
the Ideal of his holiest dreams.

In working toward such supreme accomplishment, it is
necessary to commence at the lowest and easiest steps, and
proceed by natural and progressive stages to the higher
and more difficult. This law of growth, progress, evolution,
unfoldment, by gradual and ever ascending stages, is absolute in every department of life, and in every human accomplishment, and where it is ignored, total failure will
result. In acquiring learning, in learning a trade, or in pursuing a business, this law is fully recognized and minutely
obeyed by all; but in acquiring virtue, in learning Truth,
and in pursuing the right conduct and knowledge of life, it
is unrecognized and disobeyed by nearly all; hence Virtue,
Truth, and the Perfect Life remain unpracticed, unac-
quainted, and unknown.

It is a common error to suppose that the Higher Life
is a matter of reading, and the adoption of theological or
metaphysical hypotheses, and that Spiritual Principles can
be apprehended by this method. The Higher Life is a
higher living in thought, word, and deed, and the
knowledge of those Spiritual Principles, which are imminent in man and in the universe can only be acquired
after long discipline in the pursuit and practice of Virtue.

The lesser must be thoroughly grasped and understood
before the greater can be known, the practice always
preceeds *real* knowledge. The schoolmaster never attempts to teach his pupils the abstract principles of math-
ematics at the commencement; he knows that by such a
method teaching would be vain, and learning impossible.
He first places before them a simple sum, and, having ex-
plained it, leave them to *do it*. When, after repeated

failures and ever-renewed effort, they have succeeded in doing it correctly, a more difficult task is set them, and then another and another; and not until the pupils have, through many years of diligent application, mastered all the lessons in arithmetic, does he attempt to unfold to them the underlying mathematical principles.

In learning a trade, say that of a mechanic, the boy is not at first taught the principles of mechanics, but a simple tool is put into his hand and he is told how rightly to use it, and is then left to do it by effort and practice. As he succeeds in plying his tools correctly, more and more difficult tasks are set him, until, after several years of successful practice, he is prepared to study and grasp the principles of mechanics.

In a properly governed household, the child is first taught to be obedient, and to conduct himself properly under all circumstances. The child is not even told why he must do this, but is commanded to do it, and only after he has so far succeeded in doing what is right and proper, is he told *why* he should do it. No father would attempt to teach his child the principles of ethics before exacting from him the practice of filial duty and social virtue.

Thus practice ever preceded knowledge even in the ordinary things of the world, and in spiritual things, in the living of the Higher Life, this law is rigid in its exactions. Virtue can only be known by *doing*, and the knowledge of Truth can only be arrived at by perfecting one's self in the practice of Virtue and to be complete in the practice and acquisition of Virtue is to be complete in the knowledge of Truth.

Truth can only be arrived at by daily and hourly doing the lessons of Virtue, beginning at the simplest, and passing on to the more difficult; and as a child patiently and obediently learns its lessons at school, constantly practicing, ever exerting himself until all failures and difficulties are surmounted, even so does the child of Truth apply himself to right-doing in thought and action, undaunted by failure, and made stronger by difficulties; and as he succeeds in acquiring Virtue, his mind unfolds itself in the knowledge of Truth, and it is a knowledge in which he can securely rest.

Note: This chapter originally printed in <u>Out From the Heart.</u>

CHAPTER 20

Mental Conditions and Their Effects

Every form of unhappiness springs from a
wrong condition of mind. Happiness in-
heres in right conditions of mind. Happi-
ness is mental harmony; unhappiness is
mental disharmony

Without going into the details of the greater steps and lessons in the right life (a task outside the scope of this small work) a few hints and statements concerning those mental conditions from which life in its totality springs, will prove helpful to those who are ready and willing to penetrate further into that inner realm of heart and mind where Love and Wisdom and Peace await the strenuous comer.

All sin is ignorance. It is a condition of darkness and undevelopment. The wrong-thinker and wrong-doer are in the same position in the school of life as is the ignorant pupil in the school of learning. He has yet to learn how to think and act correctly, that is, in accordance with law. The pupil in learning is not happy so long as he does his lessons wrongly, and unhappiness cannot be escaped while sin remains unconquered.

Life is a series of lessons. Some are diligent in learning them, and they become pure, wise, and altogether
happy. Others are negligent, and do not apply themselves,
and they remain impure, foolish, and unhappy.

Every form of unhappiness springs from a wrong condition of mind. Happiness inheres in right conditions of
mind. Happiness is mental harmony; unhappiness is mental disharmony. While a man lives in wrong conditions of
mind, he will live a wrong life, and will suffer continually.
Suffering is rooted in error. Bliss inheres in enlightenment. There is salvation for man only in the destruction of
his own ignorance, error, and self-delusion. Where there
are wrong conditions of mind there is bondage and unrest;
where there are right conditions of mind there is freedom
and peace.

Here are some of the leading wrong mental conditions
and their disastrous effects upon the life:

> Hatred: Injury, violence, disaster, and suffering.
> Lust: Confusion of intellect, remorse, shame,
>   and wretchedness.
> Covetousness: Fear, unrest, unhappiness, and
>   loss.
> Pride: Disappointment, chagrin, lack of
>   self-knowledge.
> Vanity: Distress, and mortification of spirit.
> Condemnation: Persecution, hatred from others.
> Ill-will: Failures and troubles.
> Self-indulgence: Misery, loss of judgment,
>   grossness, disease, and neglect.
> Anger: Loss of power and influence.
> Desire, or Self-Slavery: Grief, folly, sorrow,
>   uncertainty, and loneliness.

The above wrong conditions of mind are merely negations; they are states of darkness and deprivation and not of positive power. Evil is not a power; it is *ignorance and misuse of good*. The hater is he who has failed to do the lesson of Love correctly, and he suffers in consequence. When he succeeds in doing it rightly, the hatred will have disappeared, and he will see and understand the darkness and impotence of hatred. It is so with every wrong condition.

The following are some of the more important right mental conditions and their beneficent effects upon the life:

> Love: Gentle conditions, bliss, and blessedness.
> Purity: Intellectual clearness, joy, invincible confidence.
> Selflessness: Courage, satisfaction, happiness, and plenty.
> Humility: Calmness, restfulness, knowledge of Truth.
> Meekness: Equipoise, contentment under all circumstances.
> Compassion: Protection, love, and reverence from others.
> Good-will: Gladness and success.
> Self-control: Peace of mind, true judgment, refinement, health, and honor.
> Patience: Mental power, far-reaching influence.
> Self-conquest: Enlightenment, wisdom, insight, and profound peace.

The above right conditions of mind are states of positive power, of light, of joyful possession, and of knowledge.

The good man *knows*. He has learned to do his lessons correctly, and thereby understands the exact proportions which make up the sum of life. He is enlightened, and knows good and evil. He is supremely happy, doing only that which is divinely right.

The man who is involved in the wrong conditions of mind, does not know. He is ignorant of good and evil, of himself, of the inward causes which make his life. He is unhappy, and believes other people are entirely the cause of his unhappiness. He works blindly, and lives in darkness, seeing no central purpose in existence, and no orderly and lawful sequence in the course of things.

He who aspires to the attainment of the Higher Life in its completion — who would perceive with unveiled vision the true order of things and the meaning of life — let him abandon all the wrong conditions of heart, and persevere unceasingly in the practice of the good. If he suffers, or doubts, or is unhappy, let him search within until he finds the cause, and having found it, let him cast it away. Let him so guard and purify his heart that every day less of evil and more of good shall issue therefrom; so will he daily become stronger, nobler, wiser; so will his blessedness increase, and the Light of Truth, growing ever brighter and brighter within him, will dispel all gloom, and illuminate his Pathway.

Note: This chapter originally printed in *Out From the Heart*.

CHAPTER 21

Your World Mirrors
Your Mental State

*If circumstances had the power to bless or
harm, they would bless and harm all men
alike, but the fact that the same circumstances will be alike good and bad to different
souls proves that the good or bad is not in
the circumstance, but only in the mind of
him that encounters it.*

What you are, so is your world. Everything in the
universe is resolved into your own inward experience. It
matters little what is without, for it is all a reflection of
your own state of consciousness. It matters everything
what you are within, for everything without will be mir-
rored and colored accordingly.

All that you positively know is contained in your own
experience; all that you ever will know must pass through
the gateway of experience, and so become part of yourself.

Your own thoughts, desires, and aspirations comprise
your world, and, to you, all that there is in the universe of
beauty and joy and bliss, or of ugliness and sorrow and

pain, is contained within yourself. By your own thoughts you make or mar your life, your world, your universe. As you build within by the power of thought, so will your outward life and circumstances shape themselves accordingly. Whatsoever you harbor in the inmost chambers of your heart, will sooner or later, by the inevitable law of reaction, shape itself in your outward life. The soul that is impure, sordid and selfish, is gravitating with unerring precision towards misfortune and catastrophe; the soul that is pure, unselfish, and noble, is gravitating with equal precision towards happiness and prosperity. Every soul attracts its own, and nothing can possibly come to it that does not belong to it. To realize this is to recognize the universality of Divine Law. The incidents of every human life, which both make and mar, are drawn to it by the quality and power of its own inner thoughtlife. Every soul is a complex combination of gathered experiences and thoughts, and the body is but an improvised vehicle for its manifestation. What, therefore, your thoughts are, that is your real self; and the world around, both animate and inanimate, wears the aspect with which your thoughts clothe it. "All that we are is the result of what we have thought; it is founded on our thoughts; it is made up of our thoughts." Thus said Buddha, and it therefore follows that if a man is happy, it is because he dwells in happy thoughts; if miserable, because he dwells in despondent and debilitating thoughts. Whether one be fearful or fearless, foolish or wise, troubled or serene, within that soul lies the cause of its own state or states, and never without. And now I seem to hear a chorus of voices exclaim, "But do you really mean to say that outward circumstances do not effect our minds?" I do not say that, but I say this, and know it to be an infallible truth, *that circumstances can only affect you in so far as you allow them to do so*. You are swayed by circumstances because you have not a right understanding of the nature, use, and power of thought. You believe (and upon this little word *belief* hang all our sorrows and joys) that outward things have the power to make or mar your life; by so doing you submit to those outward things, confess that you are their slave, and they your unconditional master; by so doing, you invest them with a power which they do not, of themselves, possess, and you succumb, in reality, not to the mere circumstances, but to the gloom or gladness, the fear or hope, the strength or weakness, which your thought-sphere has thrown around them.

I knew two men who, at an early age, lost the hard-earned savings of years. One was very deeply troubled, and gave way to chagrin, worry, and despondency. The other, on reading in his morning paper that the bank in which his money was deposited had hopelessly failed, and that he had lost all, quietly and firmly remarked, "Well, it's gone, and trouble and worry won't bring it back, but hard work will." He went to work with renewed vigor and rapidly became prosperous, while the former man, continuing to mourn the loss of his money, and to grumble at his "bad luck," remained the sport and tool of adverse circumstances, the reality of his own weak and slavish thoughts. The loss of money was a curse to the one because he clothed the event with dark and dreary thoughts; it was a blessing to the other, because he threw around it thoughts of strength, of hope, and renewed endeavor.

If circumstances had the power to bless or harm, they would bless and harm all men alike, but the fact that the same circumstances will be alike good and bad to different souls proves that the good or bad is not in the circumstance, but only in the mind of him that encounters it. When you begin to realize this you will begin to control your thoughts, to regulate and discipline your mind, and to rebuild the inward temple of your soul, eliminating all useless and superfluous material, and incorporating into your being thoughts alone of joy and serenity, of strength and life, of compassion and love, of beauty and immortality; and as you do this you will become joyful and serene, strong and healthy, compassionate and loving, and beautiful with the beauty of immortality.

As we clothe events with the drapery of our own thoughts, so likewise do we clothe the objects of the visible world around us, and where one sees harmony and beauty, another sees revolting ugliness. An enthusiastic naturalist was one day roaming the country lanes in pursuit of his hobby, and during his rambles came upon a pool of brackish water near a farmyard. As he proceeded to fill a small bottle with the water for the purpose of examination under the microscope, he dilated, with more enthusiasm than discretion, to an uncultivated son of the plough who stood close by, upon the hidden and innumerable wonders contained in the pool, and concluded by saying, "yes, my friend, within this pool is contained a hundred, nay, a million universes, had we but the sense or the instrument by which we could apprehend them." And the unsophisticated one ponderously remarked, "I know the water be full o' tadpoles, but they be easy to catch."

Where the naturalist, his mind stored with the knowledge of natural facts, saw beauty, harmony, and hidden glory, the mind unenlightened upon those things saw only an offensive mud-puddle.

The wild flower which the casual wayfarer thoughtlessly tramples upon is, to the spiritual eye of the poet, an angelic messenger from the invisible. To the many, the ocean is but a dreary expanse of water on which ships sail and are sometimes wrecked; to the soul of the musician it is a living thing, and he hears, in all its changing moods, divine harmonies. Where the ordinary mind sees disaster and confusion, the mind of the philosopher sees the most perfect sequence of cause and effect, and where the materialist sees nothing but endless death, the mystic sees pulsating and eternal life.

As we clothe both events and objects with our own thoughts, so likewise do we clothe the souls of others in the garments of our thoughts. The suspicious believe everybody to be suspicious; the liar feels secure in the thought that he is not so foolish as to believe that there is such a phenomenon as a strictly truthful person; the envious see envy in every soul; the miser thinks everybody is eager to get his money; he who has subordinated conscience in the making of his wealth, sleeps with a revolver under his pillow, wrapped in the delusion that the world is full of conscienceless people who are eager to rob him, and the abandoned sensualist looks upon the saint as a hypocrite. On the other hand, those who dwell in loving thoughts, see that in all which calls forth their love and sympathy; the trusting and honest are not troubled by suspicions; the good natured and charitable who rejoice at the good fortune of others, scarcely know what envy means; and he who has realized the Divine within himself recognizes it in all beings, even in the beasts.

Men and women are confirmed in their mental outlook because of the fact that, by the law of cause and effect, they attract to themselves that which they send forth, and so come in contact with people similar to themselves. The old adage, "Birds of a feather flock together," has a deeper significance than is generally attached to it, for in the thought-world as in the world of matter, each clings to its kind.

> *"Do you wish for kindness? Be kind.*
> *Do you ask for truth? Be true.*
> *What you give of yourself you find;*
> *Your world is a reflex of you."*

If gladness for you, you may enter into and realize that happy world now; it fills the whole universe. It is within you, waiting for you to find, acknowledge and possess. Said one who knew the inner laws of Being, "When men shall say lo here, or lo there, go not after them; the kingdom of God is within you." What you have to do is to believe this, simply believe it with a mind unshadowed by doubt, and then meditate upon it till you understand it. You will then begin to purify and to build your inner world, and as you proceed, passing from revelation to revelation, from realization to realization, you will discover the utter powerlessness of outward things beside the magic potency of a self-governed soul.

Note: This chapter originally printed as Chapter 2 in The Path to Prosperity.

CHAPTER 22

Trancending Undesirable Conditions

You may bring about that improved condition in your outward life which you desire, if you will unswervingly resolve to improve your inner life.

Having seen and realized that evil is but a passing shadow thrown, by the intercepting self, across the transcendent Form of the Eternal Good, and that the world is a mirror in which each sees a reflection of himself, we now ascend, by firm and easy steps, to that plane of perception whereon is seen and realized the *Vision of the Law*. With this realization comes the knowledge that everything is included in a ceaseless interaction of cause and effect, and that nothing can possibly be divorced from law. From the most trivial thought, word, or act of man, up to the groupings of the celestial bodies, law reigns supreme. No arbitrary condition can even for one moment exist, for such a condition would be a denial and an annihilation of law. Every condition of life is, therefore, bound up in an orderly and harmonious sequence, and the secret and cause of every condition is contained within itself. The law, "Whatsoever a man sows that shall he also reap," is inscribed in flaming letters upon the portal of Eternity, and none can deny it, none can cheat it, none can escape it. He who puts his hand in the fire must suffer the burning until such time as it has worked itself out, and neither curses nor prayers can avail or alter it. And precisely the same law governs the realm of mind. Hatred, anger, jealousy, envy, lust, covetousness, all these are fires which burn, and whoever even so much as touches them must suffer the torments of burning. All these conditions of mind are rightly called "evil," for they are the efforts of the soul to subvert, in its ignorance, the law, and they, therefore, lead to chaos and confusion within, and are sooner or later actualized in the outward circumstances as disease, failure, and misfortune, coupled with grief, pain, and despair. Whereas love, gentleness, goodwill, purity, are cooling airs which breathe peace upon the soul that wooes them, and, being in harmony with the Eternal Law, they become actualized in the form of health, peaceful surroundings, and undeviating success and good fortune.

A thorough understanding of this Great Law which permeates the universe leads to the acquirement of that state of mind known as *obedience*. To know that justice, harmony, and love are supreme in the universe is likewise to know that all adverse and painful conditions are the result of our own disobedience to that Law. Such knowledge leads to strength and power, and it is upon such knowledge alone that a true life and an enduring success and happiness can be built. To be patient under all circumstances, and to accept all conditions as necessary factors in your training, is to rise superior to all painful conditions, and to overcome them with an overcoming which is sure, and which leaves no fear of their return, for by the power of obedience to law they are utterly slain. Such an obedient one is working in harmony with the law, has, in fact, identified himself with the law, and whatsoever he conquers he conquers forever; whatsoever he builds can never be destroyed.

The cause of all power, as of all weakness, is within: the secret of all happiness as of all misery is likewise within. There is no progress apart from unfoldment within, and no sure foothold of prosperity or peace except by orderly advancement in knowledge.

You say you are chained by circumstances; you cry out for better opportunities, for a wider scope, for improved physical conditions, and perhaps you inwardly curse the fate that binds you hand and foot. It is for you that I write; it is to you that I speak. Listen, and let my words burn themselves into your heart, for that which I say to you is truth: *You may bring about that improved condition in your outward life which you desire, if you will unswervingly resolve to improve your inner life.* I know this pathway looks barren at its commencement (truth always does, it is only error and delusion which are at first inviting and fascinating), but if you undertake to walk it; if you perseveringly discipline your mind, eradicating your weaknesses, and allowing your soul-forces and spiritual powers to unfold themselves, you will be astonished at the magical changes which will be brought about in your outward life. As you proceed, golden opportunities will be strewn across your path, and the power and judgment to properly utilize them will spring up within you. Genial friends will come unbidden to you; sympathetic souls will be drawn to you as the needle is to the magnet; and books and all outward aids that you require will come to you unsought.

Perhaps the chains of poverty hang heavily upon you, and you are friendless and alone, and you long with an intense longing that your load may be lightened; but the load continues, and you seem to be enveloped in an ever increasing darkness. Perhaps you complain, you bewail your lot; you blame your birth, your parents, your employer, or the unjust Powers who have bestowed upon you so undeservedly poverty and hardship, and upon another affluence and ease. Cease your complaining and fretting; none of these things which you blame are the cause of your poverty; the cause is within yourself; and where the cause is, there is the remedy. The very fact that you are a complainer, shows that you deserve your lot; shows that you lack that faith which is the ground of all effort and progress. There is no room for a complainer in a universe of law, and worry is soul-suicide. By your very attitude of mind you are strengthening the chains which bind you, and are drawing about you the darkness by which you are enveloped. Alter your outlook upon life, and your outward life will alter. Build yourself up in faith and knowledge, and make yourself worthy of better surroundings and wider opportunities. Be sure, first of all, that you are making the best of what you have. Do not delude yourself into supposing that you can step into greater advantages whilst overlooking smaller ones, for if you could, the advantage would be impermanent and you would quickly fall back again in order to learn the lesson which you had neglected. As the child at school must master one standard before passing on to the next, so, before you can have that greater good which you so desire, must you faithfully employ that which you already possess. The parable of the talents is a beautiful story illustrative of this truth, for does it not plainly show that if we misuse, neglect, or degrade that which we possess, be it ever so mean and insignificant, even that little will be taken from us, for, by our conduct we show that we are unworthy of it.

Perhaps you are living in a small cottage, and are surrounded by unhealthy vicious influences. You desire a larger and more sanitary residence. Then you must fit yourself for such a residence by first of all making your cottage as far as possible a little paradise. Keep it spotlessly clean. Make it look as pretty and sweet as your limited means will allow. Cook your plain food with all care, and arrange your humble table as tastefully as you possibly can. If you cannot afford a carpet, let your rooms be carpeted with smiles and welcomes, fastened down with the nails of kind words driven in with the hammer of patience. Such a carpet will not fade in the sun, and constant use will never wear it away.

By so ennobling your present surroundings you will rise above them, and above the need of them, and at the right time you will pass on into the better house and surroundings which have all along been waiting for you, and which you have fitted yourself to occupy.

Perhaps you desire more time for thought and effort, and feel that your hours of labor are too hard and long. Then see to it that you are utilizing to the fullest possible extent what little spare time you have. It is useless to desire more time, if you are already wasting what little you have; for you would only grow more indolent and indifferent.

Even poverty and lack of time and leisure are not the evils that you imagine they are, and if they hinder you in your progress, it is because you have clothed them in your own weaknesses, and the evil that you see in them is really in yourself. Endeavor to fully and completely realize that insofar as you shape and mold your mind, you are the maker of your destiny, and as, by the transmuting power of self-discipline you realize this more and more, you will come to see that these so-called evils may be converted into blessings. You will then utilize your poverty for the cultivation of patience, hope and courage; and your lack of time in the gaining of promptness of action and decision of mind, by seizing the precious moments as they present themselves for your acceptance. As in the rankest soil the most beautiful flowers are grown, so in the dark soil of poverty the choicest flowers of humanity have developed and bloomed. Where there are difficulties to cope with, and unsatisfactory conditions to overcome, there virtue most flourishes and manifests its glory.

It may be that you are in the employ of a tyrannous master or mistress, and you feel that you are harshly treated. Look upon this also as necessary to your training. Return your employer's unkindness with gentleness and forgiveness. Practice unceasingly patience and self-control. Turn the disadvantage to account by utilizing it for the gaining of mental and spiritual strength, and by your silent example and influence you will thus be teaching your employer, will be helping him to grow ashamed of his conduct, and will, at the same time, be lifting yourself up to that height of spiritual attainment by which you will be enabled to step into new and more congenial surroundings at the time when they are presented to you. Do not complain that you are a slave, but lift yourself up, by noble conduct, above the plane of slavery. Before complaining that you are a slave to another, be sure that you are not a slave to self. Look within; look searchingly, and have no mercy upon yourself. You will find there, perchance, slavish thoughts, slavish desires, and in your daily life and conduct slavish habits. Conquer these; cease to be a slave to self, and no man will have the power to enslave you. As you overcome self, you will overcome all adverse conditions, and every difficulty will fall before you.

Do not complain that you are oppressed by the rich. Are you sure that if you gained riches you would not be an oppressor yourself; remember that there is the Eternal Law which is absolutely just, and that he who oppresses today must himself be oppressed tomorrow; and from this there is no way of escape. And perhaps you, yesterday were rich and an oppressor, to the Great Law. Practice, therefore, fortitude and faith. Dwell constantly in mind upon the Eternal Justice, the Eternal Good. Endeavor to lift yourself above the personal and the transitory into the impersonal and permanent. Shake off the delusion that you are being injured or oppressed by another, and try to realize, by a profounder comprehension of your inner life, and the laws which govern that life, that you are only really injured by what is within you. There is no practice more degrading, debasing, and soul-destroying than of *self-pity*. Cast it out from you. While such a canker is feeding upon your heart you can never expect to grow into a fuller life. Cease from the condemnation of others, and begin to condemn yourself. Condone none of your acts, desires or thoughts that will not bear comparison with spotless purity, or endure the light of sinless good. By so doing you will be building your house upon the rock of the Eternal, and all that is required for your happiness and well being will come to you in its own time.

There is positively no way of permanently rising above poverty, or any undesirable condition, except by eradicating those selfish and negative conditions within, of which these are the reflection, and by virtue of which they continue. The way to true riches is to enrich the soul by the acquisition of virtue. Outside of real heart-virtue there is neither prosperity nor power, but only the appearances of these. I am aware that men make money who have acquired no measure of virtue, and have little desire to do so; but such money does not constitute true riches, and its possession is transitory and feverish. Here is David's testimony:

"For I was envious at the foolish when I saw the prosperity of the wicked...Their eyes stand out with fatness; they have more than heart could wish...Verily I have cleansed by heart in vain, and washed my hands in innocence...When I thought to know this it was too painful for me; until I went into the sanctuary of God, then understood I their end." (Psalms 73:3,7,13,16,17)

The prosperity of the wicked was a great trial to David until he went into the sanctuary of God, and then he *knew their end.* You likewise may go into that sanctuary. It is within you. It is that state of consciousness which remains when all that is sordid, and personal, and impermanent is risen above, and universal and eternal principles are realized. That is the God state of consciousness; it is the sanctuary of the Most High. When, by long strife and self-discipline, you have succeeded in entering the door of that holy Temple, you will perceive, with unobstructed vision, the end and fruit of all human thought and endeavor, both good and evil. You will then no longer relax your faith when you see the immoral man accumulating outward riches, for you will *know* that he must come again to poverty and degradation. The rich man who is barren of virtue is, in reality, poor, and as surely as the waters of the river are drifting to the ocean, so surely is he, in the midst of all his riches, drifting towards poverty and misfortune; and though he die rich, yet must he return to reap the bitter fruit of all his immorality. And though he become rich many times, yet as many times must he be thrown back into poverty, until, by long experience and suffering he conquers the poverty within. But the man who is outwardly poor, yet rich in virtue, is truly rich, in the midst of all his poverty, he is surely traveling towards prosperity; and abounding joy and bliss await his coming.

If you would become truly and permanently prosperous, you must first become virtuous. It is therefore unwise to aim directly at prosperity, to make it the one object of life, to reach out greedily for it. To do this is to ultimately defeat yourself. But rather aim at self-perfection, make useful and unselfish service the object of your life, and ever reach out hands of faith towards the supreme and unalterable Good.

You say you desire wealth, not for your own sake, but in order to do good with it, and to bless others. If this is your *real* motive in desiring wealth, then wealth will come to you; for you are strong and unselfish indeed if, in the midst of riches, you are willing to look upon yourself as steward and not as owner. But examine well your motive, for in the majority of instances where money is desired for the admitted object of blessing others, the real underlying motive is a love of popularity, and a desire to pose as a philantropist or reformer. If you are not doing good with what little you have, depend upon it the more money you get the more selfish you would become, and all the good you appeared to do with your money, if you attempted to do any, would be so much insinuating self-laudation. If your real desire is to do good, there is no need to wait for money before you do it; you can do it now, this very moment, and just where you are. If you are really so unselfish as you believe yourself to be, you will show it by sacrificing yourself for others now. No matter how poor you are, there is room for self-sacrifice, for did not the widow put her all into the treasury? The heart that truly desires to do good does not wait for money before doing it, but comes to the altar of sacrifice, and, leaving there the unworthy elements of self, goes out and breathes upon neighbor and stranger, friend and enemy alike, the breath of blessedness.

As the effect is related to the cause, so is prosperity and power related to the inward good, and poverty and weakness to the inward evil.

Money does not constitute true wealth, nor position, nor power, and to rely upon it alone is to stand upon a slippery place.

Your true wealth is your stock of virtue, and your true power the uses to which you put it. Rectify your heart, and you will rectify your life. Lust, hatred, anger, vanity, pride, covetousness, self-indulgence, self-seeking, obstinacy, — all gentleness, meekness, patience, compassion, generosity, self-forgetfulness, and self-renunciation, — all these are wealth and power.

As the elements of poverty and weakness are overcome, an irristible and all-conquering power is evolved from within, and he who succeeds in establishing himself in the highest virtue, brings the whole world to his feet.

But the rich, as well as the poor, have their undesirable conditions, and are frequently farther removed from happiness than the poor. And here we see how happiness depends, not upon outward aids or possessions, but upon the inward life. Perhaps you are an employer, and you have endless trouble with those whom you employ, and when you do get good and faithful employees they quickly leave you. As a result you are beginning to lose, or have completely lost, your faith in human nature. You try to remedy matters by giving better wages, and by allowing certain liberties, yet matters remain unaltered. Let me advise you. The secret of all your trouble is not in your employeess, *it is in yourself*; and if you look within, with a humble and sincere desire to discover and eradicate your error, you will, sooner or later, find the origin of all your unhappiness. It may be some selfish desire, or lurking suspicion, or unkind attitude of mind which sends out its poison upon those about you, and reacts upon yourself, even though you may not show it in your manner of speech. Think of your employees with kindness, consider their happiness and comfort, and never demand of them that extremity of service which you yourself would not care to perform were you in their place. Rare and beautiful is that humility of soul by which an employee entirely forgets himself in his employer's good; but far rarer, and beautiful with a divine beauty, is that nobility of soul by which a man, forgetting his own happiness, seeks the happiness of those who are under his authority, and who depend upon him for their bodily sustenance. And such a man's happiness is increased tenfold, nor does he need to complain of those whom he employs. Said a well-known and extensive employer of labor, who never needs to dismiss an employee: "I have always had the happiest relations with my workpeople. If you ask me how it is to be accounted for, I can only say that it has been my aim from the first to do to them as I would wish to be done by." Herein lies the secret by which all desirable conditions are secured, and all that are undesirable are overcome. Do you say that you are lonely and unloved, and have "not a friend in the world"? Then, I pray you, for the sake of your own happiness, blame nobody but yourself. Be friendly towards others, and friends will soon flock around you. Make yourself pure and lovable, and you will be loved by all.

Whatever conditions are rendering your life burdensome, you may pass out of and beyond them by developing and utilizing within you the transforming power of self-purification and self-conquest. Be it the poverty which galls (and remember that the poverty upon which I have been dilating upon is that poverty which is the source of misery, and not that voluntary poverty which is the glory of emancipated souls), or the riches which burden, or the many misfortunes, griefs, and annoyances which form the dark background in the web of life, you may overcome them by overcoming the selfish elements within which give them life.

It matters not that by the unfailing law there are past thoughts and acts to work out and to atone for, as, by the same law, we are setting in motion, during every moment of our life, fresh thoughts and acts, and we have the power to make them good or ill. Nor does it follow that if a man (reaping what he has sown) must lose money or forfeit position, that he must also lose his fortitude or forfeit his uprightness, and it is in these that his wealth and power and happiness are to be found.

He who clings to self is his own enemy, and is surrounded by enemies. He who relinquishes self is his own saviour, and is surrounded by friends like a protecting belt. Before the divine radiance of a pure heart all darkness vanishes and all clouds melt away, and he who has conquered self has conquered the universe. Come, then, out of your poverty; come out of your pain; come out of your troubles, and sighings, and complainings, and heartaches, and loneliness *by coming out of yourself*. Let the old tattered garment of your petty selfishness fall from you, and put on the new garment of universal Love. You will then realize the inward heaven, and it will be reflected in all your outward life.

He who sets his foot firmly upon the path of self-conquest, who walks, aided by the staff of Faith, the highway of self-sacrifice, will assuredly achieve the highest prosperity, and will reap abounding and enduring joy and bliss.

Note: This chapter originally printed as Chapter 3 in The Path to Prosperity.

CHAPTER 23

Thought-Forces

*Every thought you think is a force sent out,
and in accordance with its nature and intensity will it go out to seek a lodgement in
minds receptive to it, and will react upon
yourself for good or evil.*

The most powerful forces in the universe are the silent
forces; and in accordance with the intensity of its power
does a force become beneficent when rightly directed, and
destructive when wrongly employed. This is common
knowledge in regard to the mechanical forces, such as
steam, electricity, etc., but few have yet learned to apply
this knowledge to the realm of mind, where the thought-
forces (most powerful of all) are continually being
generated and sent forth as currents of salvation or
destruction.

At this stage of his evolution, man has entered into the
possession of these forces, and the whole trend of his
present advancement is their complete subjugation. All
the wisdom possible to man on this material earth is to be
found only in complete self-mastery, and the command,
"Love your enemies," resolves itself into an exhortation to

enter here and now, into the possession of that sublime wisdom by taking hold of, mastering and transmuting, those mind forces to which man is now slavishly subject, and by which he is helplessly borne, like straw on the stream, upon the currents of selfishness.

The Hebrew prophets, with their perfect knowledge of the Supreme Law, always related outward events to inward thought, and associated national disaster or success with the thoughts and desires that dominated the nation at the time. The knowledge of the causal power of thought is the basis of all their prophecies, as it is the basis of all real wisdom and power. National events are simply the working out of the psychic forces of the nation. Wars, plagues, and famines are the meeting and clashing of wrongly-directed thought-forces, the culminating points at which destruction steps in as the agent of the Law. It is foolish to ascribe war to the influence of one man, or to one body of men. It is the crowning horror of national selfishness.

It is the silent and conquering thought-forces which bring all things into manifestation. The universe grew out of thought. Matter in its last analysis is found to be merely objectivized thought. All man's accomplishments were first wrought out in thought, and then objectivized. The author, the inventor, the architect, first builds up his work in thought, and having perfected it in all its parts as a complete and harmonious whole upon the thought-plane, he then commences to materialize it, to bring it down to the material or sense-plane.

When the thought-forces are directed in harmony with the over-ruling law, they are upbuilding and preservative, but when subverted they become disintegrating and self-destructive.

To adjust all your thoughts to a perfect and unswerving faith in the omnipotence and supremacy of Good, is to cooperate with that good, and to realize within yourself the solution and destruction of all evil. *Believe and ye shall live.* And here we have the true meaning of salvation; salvation from darkness and negation of evil, by entering into, and realizing the living light of the Eternal Good.

Where there is fear, worry, anxiety, doubt, trouble, chagrin, or disappointment, there is ignorance and lack of faith. All these conditions of mind are the direct outcome of selfishness, and are based upon an inherent belief in the power and supremacy of evil; they therefore constitute practical atheism; and to live in, and become subject to these negative and soul-destroying conditions of mind is the only real atheism.

It is salvation from such conditions that the race needs, and let no man boast of salvation whilst he is their helpless and obedient slave. To fear or to worry is as sinful as to curse, for how can one fear or worry if he intrinsically believes in the Eternal Justice, the Omnipotent Good, the Boundless Love? To fear, to worry, to doubt, is to deny, to disbelieve.

It is from such states of mind that all weakness and failure proceed, for they represent the annulling and disintegrating of the positive thought-forces which would otherwise speed to their object with power, and bring about their own beneficent results.

To overcome these negative conditions is to enter into a life of power, is to cease to be a slave, and to become a master, and there is only one way by which they can be overcome, and that is by *steady and persistent growth in inward knowledge*. To mentally deny evil is not sufficient; it must be daily practiced, be risen above and understood. To mentally affirm the good is inadequate; it must, by unswerving endeavor, be entered into and comprehended.

The intelligent practice of self-control, quickly leads to a knowledge of one's interior thought-forces, and, later on, to the acquisition of that power by which they are rightly employed and directed. In the measure that you master self, that you control your mental forces instead of being controlled by them, in just such measure will you master affairs and outward circumstances.

Show me a man under whose touch everything crumbles away, and who cannot retain success even when it is placed in his hands, and I will show you a man who dwells continually in those conditions of mind which are the very negation of power. To be forever wallowing in the bogs of doubt, to be drawn continually into the quicksands of fear, or blown ceaselessly about by the winds of anxiety, is to be a slave, and to live the life of a slave, even though success and influence be forever knocking at your door seeking for admittance. Such a man, being without faith and without self-government, is incapable of the right government of his affairs, and is a slave to circumstances; in reality a slave to himself. Such are taught by affliction, and ultimately pass from weakness to strength by the stress of bitter experience.

Faith and purpose constitute the motive-power of life. There is nothing that a strong faith and an unflinching purpose may not accomplish. By the daily exercise of silent faith, the thought-forces are gathered together, and by the daily strengthening of silent purpose, those forces are directed towards the object of accomplishment.

Whatever your position in life may be, before you can hope to enter into any measure of success, usefulness, and power, you must learn how to focus your thought-forces by cultivating calmness and respose. It may be that you are a business man, and you are suddenly confronted with some overwhelming difficulty or probable disaster. You grow fearful and anxious, and are at your wit's end. To persist in such a state of mind would be fatal, for when anxiety steps in, correct judgment passes out. Now if you will take advantage of a quiet hour or two in the early morning or at night, and go away to some solitary spot, or to some room in your house where you know you will be absolutely free from intrusion, and, having seated yourself in an easy attitude, you forcibly direct your mind right away from the object of anxiety by dwelling upon something in your life that is pleasing and bliss-giving, a calm, reposeful strength will gradually steal into your mind, and your anxiety will pass away. Upon the instant that you find your mind reverting to the lower plane of worry bring it back again, and re-establish it on the plane of peace and strength. When this is fully accomplished, you may then concentrate your whole mind upon the solution of your difficulty, and what was intricate and insurmountable to you in your hour of anxiety will be made plain and easy, and you will see, with that clear vision and perfect judgment which belongs only to a calm and untroubled mind, the right course to pursue and the proper end to be brought about. It may be that you will have to try day after day before you will be able to perfectly calm your mind, but if you persevere you will certainly accomplish it. And the course which is presented to you in that hour of calmness *must be carried out*. Doubtless when you are again involved in the business of the day, and worries again creep in and begin to dominate you, you will begin to think that the course is a wrong or foolish one, but do not heed such suggestions. Be guided absolutely and entirely by the vision of calmness, and not by the shadows of anxiety. The hour of calmness is the hour of illumination and correct judgment. By such a course of mental discipline the scattered thought-forces are reunited, and directed, like the rays of the searchlight, upon the problem at issue, with the result that it gives way before them.

There is no difficulty, however great, but will yield before a calm and powerful concentration of thought, and no legitimate object but may be speedily actualized by the intelligent use and direction of one's soul-forces.

Not until you have gone deeply and searchingly into your inner nature, and have overcome the many enemies that lurk there, can you have any approximate conception of the subtle power of thought, of its inseparable relation to outward and material things, or of its magical potency, when rightly poised and directed, in readjusting and transforming the life-conditions.

Every thought you think is a force sent out, and in accordance with its nature and intensity will it go out to seek a lodgement in minds receptive to it, and will react upon yourself for good or evil. There is ceaseless reciprocity between mind and mind, and a continual interchange of thought-forces. Selfish and disturbing thoughts are so many malignant and destructive forces, messengers of evil, sent out to stimulate and augment the evil in other minds, which in turn send them back upon you with added power. While thoughts that are calm, pure, and unselfish are so many angelic messengers sent out into the world with health, healing, and blessedness upon their wings, counteracting the evil forces; pouring the oil of joy upon the troubled waters of anxiety and sorrow, and restoring to broken hearts their heritage of immortality.

Think good thoughts, and they will quickly become actualized in your outward life in the form of good conditions. Control your soul-forces, and you will be able to shape your outward life as you will. The difference between a savior and a sinner is this, that the one has a perfect control of all the forces within him; the other is dominated and controlled by them.

There is absolutely no other way to true power and abiding peace, but by self-control, self-government, self-purification. To be at the mercy of your disposition is to be impotent, unhappy, and of little real use in the world. The conquest of your petty likes and dislikes, your capricious loves and hates, your fits of anger, suspicion, jealousy, and all the changing moods to which you are more or less helplessly subject, this is the task you have before you if you would weave into the web of life the golden threads of happiness and prosperity. Insofar as you are enslaved by the changing moods within you, will you need to depend upon others and upon outward aids as you walk through life. If you would walk firmly and securely, and would accomplish any achievement, you must learn to rise above and control all such disturbing and retarding vibrations. You must daily practice the habit of putting your mind at rest, "going into the silence," as it is commonly called. This is a method of replacing a troubled thought with one of peace, a thought of weakness with one of strength. Until you succeed in doing this you cannot hope to direct your mental forces upon the problems and pursuits of life with any apreciable measure of success. It is a process of diverting one's scattered forces into one powerful channel. Just as a useless marsh may be converted into a field of golden corn or a fruitful garden by draining and directing the scattered and harmful streams into one well-cut channel, so, he who acquires calmness, and subdues and directs the thought-currents within himself, saves his soul, and fructifies his heart and life.

As you succeed in gaining mastery over your impulses and thoughts you will begin to feel, growing up within you, a new and silent power, and a settled feeling of composure and strength will remain with you. Your latent powers will begin to unfold themselves, and whereas formerly your efforts were weak and ineffectual, you will now be able to work with that calm confidence which commands success. And along with this new power and strength, there will be awakened within you that interior illumination known as "intuition," and you will walk no longer in darkness and speculation, but in light and certainty. With the development of this soul-vision, judgment and mental penetration will be incalculably increased, and there will evolve within you that prophetic vision by the aid of which you will be able to sense coming events, and to forcast, with remarkable accuracy, the result of your efforts. And in just the measure that you alter from within will your outlook upon life alter; and as you alter your mental attitude towards others they will alter in their attitude and conduct towards you. As you rise above the lower, debilitating, and destructive thought-forces, you will come in contact with the positive, strengthening, and upbuilding currents generated by strong, pure, and noble minds, your happiness will be immeasurably intensified, and you will begin to realize the joy, strength, and power, which are born only of self-mastery. And this joy, strength, and power will be continually radiating from you, and without any effort on your part, nay, though you are utterly unconscious of it, strong people will be drawn towards you, influence will be put into your hands, and in accordance with your altered thought-world will outward events shape themselves.

"A man's foes are those of his own household," and he who would be useful, strong, and happy, must cease to be a passive receptacle for the negative, beggarly, and impure streams of thought; and as a wise householder commands his servants and invites his guests, so must he learn to command his desires, and to say, with authority, what thoughts he shall admit into the mansion of his soul. Even a very partial success in self-mastery adds greatly to one's power, and he who succeeds in perfecting this divine accomplishment, enters into the possession of undreamed-of wisdom and inward strength and peace, and realizes that all the forces of the universe aid and protect his footsteps who is master of his soul.

Note: This chapter originally printed as Chapter 4 in The Path to Prosperity.

CHAPTER 24

The Power of Meditation

*Tell me what that is upon which you most
frequently and intensely think, that to
which, in your silent hours, your soul most
naturally turns, and I will tell you to what
place of pain or peace you are traveling,
and whether you are growing into the likeness of the divine or the bestial.*

Spiritual meditation is the pathway to Divinity. It is the
mystic ladder which reaches from earth to heaven, from
error to Truth, from pain to peace. Every saint has climbed
it; every sinner must sooner or later come to it, and every
weary pilgrim that turns his back upon self and the world,
and sets his face resolutely towards the Father's Home,
must plant his feet upon its golden rounds. Without its aid
you cannot grow into the divine state, the divine likeness,
the divine peace, and the fadeless glories and unpolluting
joys of Truth will remain hidden from you.

Meditation is the intense dwelling, in thought, upon an
idea or theme, with the object of thoroughly comprehend-
ing it, and whatsoever you constantly meditate upon you
will not only come to understand, but will grow more and

more into its likeness, for it will become incorporated into your very being, will become, in fact, your very self. If, therefore, you constantly dwell upon that which is selfish and debasing, you will ultimately become selfish and debased; if you ceaselessly think upon that which is pure and unselfish you will surely become pure and unselfish.

Tell me what that is upon which you most frequently and intensely think, that to which, in your silent hours, your soul most naturally turns, and I will tell you to what place of pain or peace you are traveling, and whether you are growing into the likeness of the divine or the bestial.

There is an unavoidable tendency to become literally the embodiment of that quality upon which one most constantly thinks. Let, therefore, the object of your meditation be above and not below, so that every time you revert to it in thought you will be lifted up; let it be pure and unmixed with any selfish element; so shall your heart become purified and drawn nearer to truth, and not defiled and dragged more hopelessly into error.

Meditation, in the spiritual sense in which I am now using it, is the secret of all growth in spiritual life and knowledge. Every prophet, sage, and savior became such by the power of meditation. Buddha meditated upon the Truth until he could say, "I am the Truth." Jesus brooded upon the Divine imminence until at last he could declare, "I and my Father are One."

Meditation centered upon divine realities is the very essence and soul of prayer. It is the silent reaching of the soul towards the Eternal. Mere petitionary prayer without meditation is a body without a soul, and is powerless to lift the mind and heart above sin and affliction. If you are daily praying for wisdom, for peace, for loftier purity and a fuller realization of Truth, and that for which you pray is still far from you, it means that you are praying for one thing whilst living out in thought and act another. If you will cease from such waywardness, taking your mind off those things you selfishly cling to which debar you from the possession of the stainless realities for which you pray; if you will no longer ask God to grant you that which you do not deserve, or to bestow upon you that love and compassion which you refuse to bestow upon others, but will commence to think and act in the spirit of Truth, you will day by day be growing into those realities, so that ultimately you will become one with them.

He who would secure any worldly advantage must be willing to work vigorously for it, and he would be foolish indeed who, waiting with folded hands, expected it to come to him for the mere asking. Do not then vainly imagine that you can obtain the heavenly possessions without making an effort. Only when you commence to work earnestly in the Kingdom of Truth will you be allowed to partake of the Bread of Life, and when you have, by patient and uncomplaining effort, earned the spiritual wages for which you ask, they will not be withheld from you.

If you really seek Truth, and not merely your own gratification; if you love it above all worldly pleasure and gains; more, even, than happiness itself, you will be willing to make the effort necessary for its achievement.

If you would be freed from sin and sorrow; if you would taste of that spotless purity for which you sigh and pray; if you would realize wisdom and knowledge, and would enter into the possession of profound and abiding peace, come now and enter the path of meditation, and let the supreme object of your meditation be Truth.

At the outset, meditation must be distinguished from *idle reverie*. There is nothing dreamy and unpractical about it. It is *a process of searching and uncompromising thought which allows nothing to remain but the simple and naked truth*. Thus meditating you will no longer strive to build yourself up in your prejudices, but, forgetting self, you will remember only that you are seeking the Truth. And so you will remove, one by one, the errors which you have built around yourself in the past, and will patiently wait for the revelation of Truth which will come when your errors have been sufficiently removed. In the silent humility of your heart you will realize that;

> "There is an inmost center in us all
>   Where Truth abides in fulness; and around,
>   Wall upon wall, the gross flesh hems it in;
>   This perfect, clear perception, which is Truth,
>   A baffling and perverting carnal mesh
>   Blinds it, and makes all error; and to know,
>   Rather consists in opening out a way
>   Whence the imprisoned splendor may escape,
>   Than in effecting entry for a light
>   Supposed to be without."

Select some portion of the day in which to meditate, and keep that period sacred to your purpose. The best time is the very early morning when the spirit of repose is upon everything. All natural conditions will then be in your favor; the passions, after the long bodily fast of the night, will be subdued, the excitements and worries of the previous day will have died away, and the mind, strong and yet restful, will be receptive to spiritual instruction. Indeed, one of the first efforts you will be called upon to make will be to shake off lethargy and indulgence, and if you refuse you will be unable to advance, for the demands of the spirit are imperative.

To be spiritually awakened is also to be mentally and physically awakened. The sluggard and the self-indulgent can have no knowledge of Truth. He who, possessed of health and strength, wastes the calm, precious hours of the silent morning in drowsy indulgence is totally unfit to climb the heavenly heights.

He whose awakening consciousness has become alive to its lofty possibilities, who is beginning to shake off the darkness of ignorance in which the world is enveloped, rises before the stars have ceased their vigil, and, grappling with the darkness within his soul, strives, by holy aspiration, to perceive the light of Truth while the unawakened world dreams on.

> "The heights by great men reached and kept,
>   Were not attained by sudden flight,
>   But they, while their companions slept,
>   Were toiling upward in the night."

No saint, no holy man, no teacher of Truth ever lived who did not rise early in the morning. Jesus habitually rose early, and climbed the solitary mountains to engage in holy communion. Buddha always rose an hour before sunrise and engaged in meditation, and all his disciples were enjoined to do the same.

If you have to commence your daily duties at a very early hour, and are thus debarred from giving the early morning to systematic meditation, try to give an hour at night, and should this, by the length and laboriousness of your daily task be denied you, you need not despair, for you may turn your thoughts upward in holy meditation in the intervals of your work or in those few idle minutes which you now waste in aimlessness; and should your work be of that kind which becomes by practice automatic, you may meditate while engaged upon it. That eminent Christian saint and philosopher, Jacob Boehme, realized his vast knowledge of divine things whilst working long hours as a shoemaker. In every life there is time to think, and the busiest, the most laborious is not shut out from aspiration and meditation.

Spiritual meditation and self-discipline are inseparable; you will, therefore, commence to meditate upon yourself so as to try and understand yourself, for remember, the great object you will have in view will be the complete removal of all your errors in order that you may realize Truth. You will begin to question your motives, thoughts, and acts, comparing them with your ideal, and endeavoring to look upon them with a calm, and impartial eye. In this manner you will be continually gaining more of that mental and spiritual equilibrium without which men are but helpless straws upon the ocean of life. If you are given to hatred or anger you will meditate upon gentleness and forgiveness, so as to become acutely alive to a sense of your harsh and foolish conduct. You will then begin to dwell in thoughts of love, of gentleness, of abounding forgiveness; and as you overcome the lower by the higher, there will gradually, silently steal into your heart a knowledge of the divine Law of Love with an understanding of its bearing upon all the intricacies of life and conduct. And in applying this knowledge to your every thought, word, and act, you will grow more and more gentle, more and more loving, more and more divine. And thus every error, every selfish desire, every human weakness, by the power of meditation is overcome. And as each sin, each error is thrust out, a fuller and clearer measure of the Light of Truth illumines the pilgrim soul.

Thus meditating, you will be ceaselessly fortifying yourself against your only *real* enemy, your selfish, perishable self, and will be establishing yourself more and more firmly in the divine and imperishable self that is inseparable from Truth. The direct outcome of your meditations will be a calm, spiritual strength which will be your stay and resting-place in the struggle of life. Great is the overcoming power of holy thought, and the strength and knowledge gained in the hour of silent meditation will enrich the soul with saving remembrance in the hour of strife, of sorrow or of temptation.

As, by the power of meditation, you grow in wisdom, you will relinquish, more and more, your selfish desires which are fickle, impermanent, and productive of sorrow and pain; and will take your stand, with increasing steadfastness and trust, upon unchangeable principles, and will realize heavenly rest.

The use of meditation is the acquirement of a knowledge of eternal principles, and the power which results from meditation is the ability to rest upon and trust those principles, and so become one with the Eternal. The end of meditation is, therefore, direct knowledge of Truth, God, and the realization of divine and profound peace.

Let your meditations take their rise from the ethical ground which you now occupy. Remember that you are to *grow* into Truth by steady perseverance. If you are an orthodox Christian, meditate ceaselessly upon the spotless purity and divine excellence of the character of Jesus, and apply his every precept to your inner life and outward conduct, so as to approximate more and more towards his perfection. Do not be as those religious ones, who, refusing to meditate upon the Law of Truth, and to put into practice the precepts given to them by their Master, are content to formally worship, to cling to their particular creeds, and to continue in the ceaseless round of sin and suffering. Strive to rise, by the power of meditation, above all selfish clinging to partial gods or party creeds; above dead formalities and lifeless ignorance. Thus walking the highway of wisdom, with mind fixed upon the spotless Truth, you shall know no halting-place short of the realization of Truth.

He who earnestly meditates first perceives a truth, as it were, afar off, and then realizes it by daily practice. It is only the doer of the Word of Truth that can know of the doctrine of Truth, for though by pure thought the Truth is perceived, it is only actualized by practice.

Said the divine Gautama, the Buddha, "He who gives himself up to vanity, and does not give himself up to meditation, forgetting the real aid of life and grasping at pleasure, will in time envy him who has exerted himself in meditation," and he instructed his disciples in the following "Five Great Meditations":

"The first meditation is the meditation of love, in which you so adjust your heart that you long for the weal and welfare of all beings, including the happiness of your enemies.

"The second meditation is the meditation of pity, in which you think of all beings in distress, vividly representing in your imagination their sorrow and anxieties so as to arouse a deep compassion for them in your soul.

"The third meditation is the meditation of joy, in which you think of the prosperity of others, and rejoice with their rejoicings.

"The fourth meditation is the meditation of impurity, in which you consider the evil consequences of corruption, the effects of sin and diseases. How trivial often is the pleasure of the moment, and how fatal its consequences.

"The fifth meditation is the meditation on serenity, in which you rise above love and hate, tyranny and oppression, wealth and want, and regard your own fate with impartial calmness and perfect tranquility."

By engaging in these meditations the disciples of the Buddha arrived at a knowledge of the Truth. But whether you engage in these particular meditations or not matters little so long as your object is Truth, so long as you hunger and thirst for that righteousness which is a holy heart and a blameless life. In your meditations, therefore, let your heart grow and expand with everbroadening love, until, freed from all hatred, and passion, and condemnation, it embraces the whole universe with thoughtful tenderness. As the flower opens its petals to receive the morning light, so open your soul more and more to the glorious light of Truth. Soar upward upon the wings of aspiration; be fearless, and believe in the loftiest possibilities. Believe that a life of absolute meekness is possible; believe that a life of stainless purity is possible; believe that a life of perfect holiness is possible; believe that the realization of the highest truth is possible. He who so believes, climbs rapidly the heavenly hills, whilst the unbelievers continue to grope darkly and painfully in the fog-bound valleys.

So believing, so aspiring, so meditating, divinely sweet and beautiful will be your spiritual experiences, and glorious the revelations that will enrapture your inward vision. As you realize the divine Love, the divine Justice, the divine Purity, the Perfect Law of Good, or God, great will be your bliss and deep your peace. Old things will pass away, and all things will become new. The veil of the material universe, so dense and impenetrable to the eye of error, so thin and gauzy to the eye of Truth, will be lifted and the spiritual universe will be revealed. Time will cease, and you will live only in Eternity. Change and mortality will no more cause you anxiety and sorrow, for you will become established in the unchangeable, and will dwell in the very heart of immortality.

Note: This chapter originally printed as Chapter 1 in The Way of Peace.

CHAPTER 25

The Realization of Perfect Peace

*If, O reader! you would realize the Light
that never fades, the Joy that never ends,
and the tranquility that cannot be disturbed; then conquer yourself. Bring every
thought, every impulse, every desire into perfect obedience to the divine power resident
within you. There is no other way to peace
but this.*

In the external universe there is ceaseless turmoil, change, and unrest; at the heart of all things there is undisturbed repose; in this deep silence dwelleth the Eternal.

Man partakes of this duality, and both the surface change and disquietude, and the deep-seated eternal abode of Peace are contained within him.

As there are silent depths in the ocean which the fiercest storm cannot reach, so there are silent, holy depths in the heart of man which the storms of sin and sorrow can never disturb. To reach this silence and to live consciously in it is peace.

Discord is rife in the outward world, but unbroken harmony holds sway at the heart of the universe. The human soul, torn by discordant passion and grief, reaches blindly towards the harmony of the sinless state, and to reach this state and to live consciously in it is peace.

Hatred severs human lives, fosters persecution, and hurls nations into ruthless war, yet men, though they do not understand why, retain some measure of faith in the overshadowing of a Perfect Love; and to reach this Love and to live consciously in it is peace.

And this inward peace, this silence, this harmony, this Love, is the Kingdom of Heaven, which is so difficult to reach because few are willing to give up themselves and to become as little children.

> "Heaven's gate is very narrow and minute,
> It cannot be perceived by foolish men
> Blinded by vain illusions of the world;
> Even the clear-sighted who discern the way,
> And seek to enter, find the portal barred,
> And hard to be unlocked. Its massive bolts
> Are pride and passion, avarice and lust."

Men cry peace! peace! where there is no peace, but on the contrary, discord, disquietude and strife. Apart from the Wisdom which is inseparable from self-renunciation, there can be no real and abiding peace.

The peace which results from social comfort, passing gratification, or worldly victory is transitory in its nature, and is burned up in the heat of the fiery trial. Only the Peace of Heaven endures through all trial, and only the selfless heart can know the Peace of Heaven.

Holiness alone is the undying peace. Self-control leads to it, and the ever-increasing Light of Wisdom guides the pilgrim on his way. It is partaken of in a measure as soon as the path of virtue is entered upon, but it is only realized in its fulness when self disappears in the consumation of a stainless life.

> "This is peace,
> To conquer love of self and lust of life,
> To tear deep-rooted passion from the heart
> To still in inward strife."

If, O reader! you would realize the Light that never fades, the Joy that never ends, and the tranquility that cannot be disturbed; if you would leave behind forever your sins, your sorrows, your anxieties and perplexities; if, I say, you would partake of this salvation, this supremely glorious Life, then conquer yourself. Bring every thought, every impulse, every desire into perfect obedience to the divine power resident within you. There is no other way to peace but this, and if you refuse to walk it, your much praying and your strict adherence to ritual will be fruitless and unavailing, and neither gods nor angels can help you. Only to him that overcometh is given the white stone of the regenerate life, on which is written the New and Ineffable Name.

Come away, for a while, from external things, from the pleasures of the senses, from the arguments of the intellect, from the noise and the excitements of the world, and withdraw yourself into the inmost chamber of your heart, and there, free from the sacrilegious intrusion of all selfish desires, you will find a deep silence, a holy calm, blissful repose, and if you will rest awhile in that holy place, and will meditate there, the faultless eye of Truth will open within you, and you will see things as they really are. This holy place within you is your real and eternal self; it is the divine within you; and only when you identify yourself with it can you be said to be "clothed and in your right mind." It is the abode of peace, the temple of wisdom, the dwelling-place of immortality. Apart from this inward resting-place, this Mount of Vision, there can be no true peace, no knowledge of the Divine, and if you can remain there for one minute, one hour, or one day, it is possible for you to remain there always.

All your sins and sorrows, your fears and anxieties are your own, and you can cling to them or you can give them up. Of your own accord you can come to abiding peace. No one else can give up sin for you; you must give it up yourself. The greatest teacher can do no more than walk the way of Truth for himself, and point it out to you; you yourself must walk it for yourself. You can obtain freedom and peace alone by your own efforts, by yielding up that which binds the soul, and which is destructive of peace.

The angels of divine peace and joy are always at hand, and if you do not see them, and hear them, and dwell with them, it is because you shut yourself out from them, and prefer the company of the spirits of evil within you. You are what you will to be, what you wish to be, what you prefer to be. You can commence to purify yourself, and by so doing can arrive at peace, or you can refuse to purify yourself, and so remain with suffering.

Step aside, then; come out of the fret and the fever of life; away from the scorching heat of self, and enter the inward resting-place where the cooling airs of peace will calm, renew, and restore you.

Come out of the storms of sin and anguish. Why be troubled and tempest-tossed when the haven of peace is so near?

Give up all self-seeking; give up self, and lo! the Peace of God is yours!

Subdue the animal within you; conquer every selfish uprising, every discordant voice; transmute the base metals of your selfish nature into the unalloyed gold Love, and you shall realize the Life of Perfect Peace. Thus subduing, thus conquering, thus transmuting, you will, O reader! whilst living in the flesh, cross the dark waters of mortality, and will reach the Shore upon which the storms of sorrow never beat, and where sin and suffering and dark uncertainty cannot come. Standing upon that Shore, holy, compassionate, awakened, and self-possessed and glad with unending gladness, you will realize that:

> "Never the Spirit was born, the Spirit will cease
>   to be never;
>   Never was time it was not, end and beginning are
>   dreams;
>   Birthless and deathless and changeless
>   remaineth the Spirit forever;
>   Death hath not touched it at all, dead though the
>   house of it seems."

You will then know the meaning of Sin, of Sorrow, of Suffering, and that the end thereof is Wisdom; will know the cause and the issue of existence.

And with this realization you will enter into rest, for this is the bliss of immortality, this the unchangeable gladness, this the untrammeled knowledge, undefiled Wisdom, and undying Love; this, and this only, is the realization of Perfect Peace.

Note: This chapter was originally published as the last chapter in The Way of Peace.

OTHER PRODUCTS FROM MINDART

AS A MAN THINKETH – Mini-Book & Audiocassette

The entire text of the million seller by James Allen on audio cassette, professionally narrated, and a handy mini pocket book for frequent review of this inspiring message of the mental laws which lead to a calm, contented and peaceful inner life.

81192-04 – $8.95 US

SELF RELIANCE – Audiocassette

This classic essay by Ralph Waldo Emerson declares the divine voice within our souls as the source of our wisdom and the practice of self-reliance as the first law of true progression and success. One hour audio cassette.

81192-03 – $6.95 US

THE POCKET COMPANION of Inspirational Thought –

A revolutionary new type of book–a reread book–scientifically designed to be lived with. It's small size (only 4 inches by 2 3/4 inches) allows you to carry it with you wherever you go and take advantage of spare moments to invest in your mind. Over 100 pages containing 516 inspirational thoughts from the world's greatest thinkers and doers. Instant inspiration. A pocket university.

81192-02 – $3.95 US

AS A MAN THINKETH, VOLUME 2 –

A glorious companion volume for the millions who have loved and profited by James Allen's original As A Man Thinketh. This inspirational self-help book makes for perfect gift giving. 146 pages, trade paperback.

81192-00 – $7.95 US

Available at your local bookstore or you can order direct:

Send your order to: MindArt Publishing
P.O. Box 641
Bountiful, Utah 84010
Tel. (801)292-1807

To provide fast and accurate processing of your order please do the following:

1. List the title(s) you would like with appropriate code number and quantity for each title.

2. Total the amount of your order and add $1.00 US for shipping and handling on first title and 50 cents for each additional title. Utah residents add 6 1/4% sales tax.

3. Enclose a check or money order for the amount of your order.

4. Enclose the shipping address you want your order sent to.

5. Send your order to the above address. Please allow 3-4 weeks for delivery.

The mind is made up of what it feeds upon. – William James